ABSINTHE

THE
EXQUISITE
ELIXIR

Nineteenth-century stills in the Combier distillery, Saumur, France

ABSINTHE

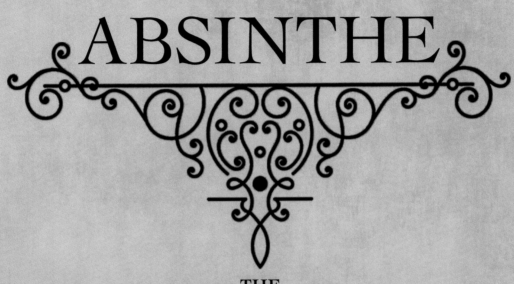

THE
EXQUISITE
ELIXIR

written by
BETINA J. WITTELS, MS Ed
and
T.A. BREAUX

Library of Congress Cataloging-in-Publication Data

Names: Wittels, Betina J., author. | Breaux, T. A., author.
Title: Absinthe : the exquisite elixir / Betina J. Wittels, T.A. Breaux.
Description: Golden, CO : Fulcrum Publishing, 2017.
Identifiers: LCCN 2016047036 | ISBN 9781682750018 (paperback)
Subjects: LCSH: Absinthe. | Absinthe--Social aspects. | Drinking
    customs--History. | BISAC: COOKING / Beverages / Wine & Spirits. | COOKING
    / History.
Classification: LCC GT2898 .W58 2017 | DDC 394.1/3--dc23
LC record available at https://lccn.loc.gov/2016047036

Fulcrum Publishing has made its best efforts to locate and credit original sources for the artwork used in this book. Please contact us if we have made any errors or omissions.
Photo credits: From the collection of T.A. Breaux (ii, 9 [lower right], 24, 33, 51, 54, 56, 58 [left and inset], 64, 68, 69, 72, 84, 99, 119, 120–136); From the collection of JBN (xii, 8, 40, 41, 103); Private collection (3, 9 [upper right], 15, 35, 42, 61, 74, 90, 92, 96, 114); From the collection of Betina Wittels (vi, viii, 1, 5 [left], 13, 14, 21, 22, 25, 29 [right], 32, 34, 37, 44, 47, 48, 49, 50, 55, 66 [right], 67, 73 [right], 77 [left], 78 [inset], 79 [right], 82 [lower left and right], 85 [left and center bottles], 86 [right], 88 [top], 98, 100 [lower left], 113, 116, 117); Maison Premiere (viii); Maxwell Britten (x); From the collection of Cary René Bonnecaze (xiv, 5 [right], 11, 29 [left], 30, 38, 43, 45, 46, 52, 58 [right], 59, 60, 62, 63, 66 [upper and lower left], 70, 73 [left], 76, 77 [right], 78, 79 [glasses], 80, 81, 82 [top left], 83, 85 [right bottle], 86 [left], 87, 88 [bottom], 89, 91, 93, 94–95, 100 [top], 101, 102, 104, 106, 118); Shutterstock. com (Everett Historical, 6; Grey Tree Studios, 7; Charlesimage, 10; Everett-Art, 16, 17; Boris15, 20; Gutzemberg, 53; Paul Schlemmer, 71); Alamy (Artepics, xvi; Heritage Image Partnership Ltd., 2, 12; Peter Horree, 4; Masterpics, 18; Chronicle, 19; John Norman, 28; Pictorial Press Ltd., 31); From the collection of David Clemmer (26, 39, 57).

Fulcrum Publishing
4690 Table Mountain Dr., Ste. 100
Golden, CO 80403
800-992-2908 • 303-277-1623
www.fulcrum-books.com

Dedication

This book is dedicated to the late Mike Iavarone, for without his guidance this absinthe journey would never have begun. I could never even whisper that this book was inspired by me alone. Adventurous as I am, this book would have never come to exist without the beings named hereafter. Besides the Green Fairy, who literally flung me into her realm and traipsed next to me through more than several continents, barrios, pueblos, bodegas, brocantes, markets, and villages, are those who led, nudged, comforted, taught, and helped me in every possible way. To these friends, mentors, customers, associates, collectors, dealers, and guides, I offer my humble gratitude.

– Betina J. Wittels, MS Ed

This book would not have been possible without the assistance of Samantha Bonar, Franck Choisne, Jared Gurfein, Peter Schaf, Jenny Gardener, my friends and associates from around the globe, and the enduring patience of my wonderful family.

– T.A. Breaux

Acknowledgments

A special thank you to Cary René Bonnecaze for the countless antiques and photos he provided, as well as the time he spent helping us bring the book to publication.

Additional thanks to:

François Bezençon • B.J. Bordelon • Ray Bordelon • Eric Brempell • Susan Brown • Paolo Castellano • Ryan Clark • David Clemmer • Patrice Cordier • Bernard Cousin • Aaron DeFoe • Jill DeGroff • François Guy • Nicole Hanson • Mike Iavarone • Nick Letson • Eric Longuet • Peggy Martin • Norman Nichols • Dan Noreen • Patrick O'Connor • Chris Peery • Father Patrick J. Perez • Eric Przygocki • Steve Rosat • Jennifer Shelton • Ana Strecyzn • Monica and Claude Talluel • Tracy Thomas • Diane Tripet • Matthias Wohlwend • God, and the Green Fairy

CONTENTS

Opposite: One of four black cat postcards that promote the allegedly docile quality of Absinthe Bourgeois

FOREWORD Maxwell Britten

When I was younger, I was lucky enough to have friends who had cultivated a taste for quality, or at least what we thought were the finer things. At the young age of eighteen, in between watching Ian Curtis biopics and collecting post-punk records, we discovered a vendor in the Czech Republic who was selling homemade absinthe kits. After mailing a handwritten money order to somewhere in Europe and a two-month wait, our kit finally arrived. At the time, we thought we were onto something. Even now, I can't adequately express what exactly happened after we drank it. Let's just say those absinthe kits were nothing but cheap, high proof alcohol with skimpy bags of dried herbs and licorice. We were drinking the wrong "absinthe," and we were drinking it the wrong way.

My taste for real absinthe evolved only with my maturity. In retrospect, it's amusing to reflect on everything I didn't know about absinthe, considering the volume of knowledge I would eventually accrue.

My father is a restaurateur, which means I grew up in restaurants. I started to put in my time behind the bar while simultaneously developing a personal relationship with art and culture. To me, these two worlds were separate and compartmentalized. I barbacked and bussed tables so I could support my habit of books, records, and crazy absinthe kits. And that first sip of our homemade "absinthe" – the most intense and blinding firewater I'd ever tasted – was enough of a fiery inspiration for me to plant myself in New York City, that ocean of history and pop culture in which I had to immerse myself. After only a short time in the city, I encountered places that were beginning to take the craft of the cocktail more seriously. I saw people make drinks with precision and technical prowess. There was a level of ceremony occurring behind the bar that I'd never before witnessed, and it spoke to me like nothing else had. I began making the connection that pop culture, art, and what I did to pay the bills were not mutually exclusive. My interest in literature shifted to reprints of antique cocktail manuals, and books focused on spirits, bars, and cocktails. I became obsessed.

As I continued to study and hone my bar skills, the subject of absinthe continued to surface. It was always called for in vintage recipes and "must know" drinks such as the Sazerac, but only in scant amounts – a couple of drops here and a rinse there. Occasionally I would have customers who'd spent time abroad come into my bar and ask for absinthe, served "Czech style" (flamed). Being someone who tries to avoid the word "no," I aimed to please, but something still seemed off. When I was asked to

Opposite: The bar at Maison Premiere, Brooklyn, New York

 ix

serve absinthe this way, the reasoning behind these steps of service always baffled me. Most of the time I was doing this with pastis or some other absinthe

alternative, as the genuine article wasn't legal in the United States. Soon after these episodes of fire and vapor, genuine absinthe was relegalized after being

banned for almost a century. Yet even when we finally got the real McCoy, most people still didn't know what to do with it or how to order it, and the charade continued.

Absinthe had been stigmatized by its ban and its own nebulous history. This became problematic in the late twentieth century, when many faux versions of it were sold as illicit, evil, and hallucinatory elixirs to anyone willing to be coaxed into a shot of high proof alcohol, set on fire. But once absinthe was legal and available, many people in the United States had loads of questions. As a bartender who was trying to take my work seriously, I had to get the answers, and they weren't easy to come by in the early days.

One by one, more absinthes became available in the United States, some even produced locally in Washington, California, New York, and Colorado. As a drinking society, we were slowly learning the truths of absinthe; primarily what it represented in the past and honoring it in the way that the French had originally intended. It was a drink that was meant to be surrounded by ceremony, art, and conversation.

At this time, I was approached by two gents who had the idea to open a bar that no one in this century had yet thought of: an absinthe bar with the largest selection of proper absinthe in the country. Inspired by trips to France and New Orleans, where I studied the essence of absinthe and absinthe-drinking culture down to infinitesimal detail, this became my calling. I knew I had to be a part of it, so as a team we created Maison Premiere and we opened at the beginning of 2011.

More than twenty-eight varieties of absinthe sat on the back bar, not including my personal shelf of "individually imported" absinthe in the back. The beautiful labels and bottles of all different shapes and sizes populated the ornate stage we built to revere the mysterious spirit we held in high regard.

The bar we built was intended for beauty and opulence, but there was substance to the experience we were invoking. We wanted to set the record straight. We wanted people to ask these questions. People did. The environment was one of hospitality, encouraging people to learn about, enjoy, and honor the absinthe that was the centerpiece of one of the most influential communities of art and culture. While most bars would stock maybe a couple bottles of absinthe and let them collect dust between long pauses of a dash here and rinse there in cocktails, we were driving volume on every bottle. We had the world's attention. We were bringing back a dead category and could not have been more proud to do so. Within a year of our opening, absinthe had gone from obsolescence to mainstream.

In 2014, I was invited by an award-winning wine director to lead an absinthe training session at Eleven Madison Park – considered by some to be the third best restaurant in the world, and the best restaurant in North America. Within three years of launching Maison Premiere, I was standing before some of the most respected and accomplished people in my industry, who were now my peers. At this point, influential people were recognizing absinthe as a category unto itself and here to stay. They wanted to participate in getting its story right too.

The modern American palate is not one for the lip-smacking, herbaceous flavor profile absinthe can often embody, but we are evolving. Americans care about what products they consume. We want to discover, to be informed, and we like a good story. Absinthe delivers these things in aces. We are in a revolutionary period of discovery, and in the last five years, the category of absinthe has multiplied because of it.

Absinthe invites us to remember the ritual of conversation and community. Although the drink dates to the eighteenth century, it is in a constant state of exploration, categorized affectionately as a consummate person of interest. Don't take it from me; pick up a bottle of an absinthe verte, ice some water, put on your favorite record, and let the Green Fairy do the rest.

Maxwell Britten

Co-founder of The Liquor Cabinet
Managing Partner of The Django NYC
Former Bar Director of Maison Premiere

Opposite: Maxwell Britten

Seule celle que nous voyons
ne sont pas jollie comme
celle la

INTRODUCTION Betina J. Wittels

EXQUISITE. My ears are mesmerized by the word's timbre. The sound is simultaneously crisp, intricate, ornate, mysterious, yet tightly woven. That word describes absinthe. It is easy to meander in poetry about absinthe. The muse is near. Sipping Suisse La Bleue as I inscribe these words I am compelled to describe the sensory experience. The louched liquid looks like blue sky on a winter day, tastes like a wispy cloud, and transports my spirit to the Garden of Eden before the serpent showed up! That is the essence of the experience of absinthe: Innocence. That is how I was fifteen years ago when I began the search for the elusive, yet exquisite elixir. To this day one may wander into a tiny Swiss village and meet a farmer approximately sixty to eighty years old who will beckon one into a secret room in his home to sip the elixir. Anything is possible with absinthe.

How time and experience transform us! Fear, intrigue, insanity, and violence lurked around the word *absinthe* for almost a hundred years, since the ban. I had to alleviate fears and persuade with eloquence to convince anyone to consider, let alone sip, the liquid. Now mainstream, the characterizing emotions of newbies are curiosity, excitement, and desire. The cape of evil has been lifted off the pure and delightful experience of imbibing absinthe. I retell my initiation story below in a briefer version than my prior book, before I bring you into 2017, ten years after the ban was removed.

"Our lives are never entirely our own. Detours of destiny are everywhere..." Thirteen years after I inscribed those words in *Absinthe: Sip of Seduction* I still submit myself to the same philosophy of life. Life is cyclical with ebbs and flows like the waxing and waning crescent moon. But the outline of each star's constellation remains embedded in the night sky even if not quite in the same location. Just move the eyes a little and there still shines the stunning Milky Way! Although it seems like a century has passed since that fateful evening, I distinctly recall the misty, naked November chill wrapping itself around me like a dark velvet cloak. It was the eve of my first encounter with absinthe.

I can still see that ominous, dimly lit path into El Raval, Barcelona, where I sat squinting through the foggy taxi window. Only moments before I had stepped into that taxi and whispered the address request in Spanish... the driver nodded and drove off in silence. As we approached the narrow *calle*, where hookers and thieves lurked in the drizzly shadows, he turned hesitantly to me and politely voiced a refusal to cross over the major street of Las Ramblas and into the lamplit alley.

Opposite: The handwriting on this postcard promoting Rivoire Absinthe claims, "All the girls we see are not as pretty as this one."

 xiii

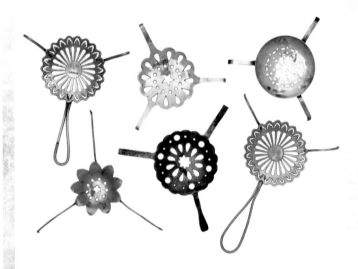

Top: A balancier set used for a single serving of absinthe. Water is poured into the cone, and then flows out onto a lever. The water flow creates a see-saw movement to dispense the water onto a piece of sugar.

Bottom: An assortment of antique grille style absinthe spoons

While I understood and perhaps even agreed with him, I knew this would be my last chance. Tomorrow I would depart to return to the United States. Meanwhile, simmering in my thoughts was the discovery I made only a few days before when, as my eyes swept through an obscure travel book, my soul lingered upon a single passage that described an elusive, mysterious green elixir, a potion banned almost worldwide, yet occasionally tippled in the Barcelona underworld, poured into odd-shaped glasses and diluted with water that trickled through sugar lumps resting on slotted spoons. It would only be here, at this particular bar situated in a very perilous section of town, that I might procure this apparently magical liquor. This peculiar vision clenched my imagination with a relentless grip.

There I was, peering through that taxi window, faced with a vexing prospect of having to go the final distance alone. If I stepped outside the taxi, I would become rain drenched while navigating my way through the shadows. It was midnight, the tumultuous time when the bars of Catalonia are reverberating with decadence. After all, nobody in Barcelona slumbers until at least 4:00 a.m. after a strong dose of Saturday night revelry. I begged the driver to creep forward, threatening to step out and walk the remaining three blocks myself. The driver demanded that I must lock my passenger door if he was going to continue. Admittedly, for a moment, my resolve stumbled. Turning back, however, is not in my nature. So I did as he asked and locked the door. I was quietly thankful, as I reminded myself that at least he had not pushed me out the door.

His instincts of machismo eventually prevailed, and, after he mustered a bit of courage, we slowly pushed forward. He parked directly in front of a huge, slatted wooden door. No other cars were in sight. "Is it even open?" I murmured to myself. The entryway at the corner of Sant Pau #65 did not look like any bar I could recall or would even want to remember. We stepped out and peered between the wooden planks. The shutters were tightly closed, but slight reverberations of rock music rattled the windows. The taxi driver reluctantly escorted me into Bar Marsella, though he was obviously tempted to abandon me in favor of guarding his taxi from the possible attacks of wheel thieves.

On a dusty barstool in a room with pink walls, beneath a dangling crystal chandelier riddled with burnt-out bulbs, I partook of my first sip of Absenta Lasala. I remember it well, sipping the elixir amidst an ambiance of uncertainty. The lights flickered; the spoon clinked against the glass. The bar was not what I expected, although looking back I cannot recall just what I had anticipated.

My life has never been the same since that moment. Enchanted, I fell under the spell, not knowing that absinthe would become for me an abode of passion. Having stepped through the entrancing absinthe door, I happened into a mystical world of herbs, forests, bistro cafés, elegantly etched glasses, shimmering topettes, embossed fountains, and intricately shaped sipping accoutrements of which, prior to that first primeval night, I knew nothing. I was equally oblivious to the history, art, literature, poetry, antiques, and passion that encircle absinthe.

The history and art that surround the drink had been explored by only a scant handful of authors, most of whom concentrated exclusively on its rich, sordid past and, to a lesser extent, depictions of absinthe in art and the century-old antiques associated with the elixir's preparation.

This particular book is intended to be a sublime, yet also practical, guide, written for both present imbibers and those curious souls who are wondering what absinthe is and if its reputation is as mysteriously powerful as the unique liquor has enticingly vowed.

T.A. Breaux and I believe that the quest for absinthe knowledge does not culminate in a dead end, but rather continues as an upwardly winding path in which fairies, poetry, and vision inspire the spirit, quench the body, and soothe the soul. Absinthe is still a fairy tale with real beginnings and no end. Thirteen years since that first book the journey now flies up and forward unfettered by demons of ignorance and insanity. Absinthe has risen from the embers of near death. The fairy glows bright in the night's starry sky.

I am excited and honored that I have been asked to revise my first book on absinthe. I hold up a glass of the mystical elixir and toast to you, the reader and, perhaps, imbiber, of this magical and potent potion.

Betina J. Wittels, MS Ed.

1

EXQUISITE
to the
Eye and Mind

Absinthe is a word that invokes a cacophony of sordid imagery and anecdotes. The liquor itself carries a legacy as a bohemian panacea – one that is praised and demonized in written works and immortalized in imagery. There has been a shared belief through history that the Green Fairy inspired artists and writers alike to bursts of creative genius as a reward to those willing to step into her world.

Absinthe is forever immortalized in the colorful writings of those who found themselves seduced by its power to fuel creativity, a virtue with which it was often credited. And in the pigments and paints that one glimpses across the passage of time and through the harsh lens of reality, haunting figures emerge from the past, illustrating the full palette of color associated with the café culture of the Belle Époque – the Beautiful Period.

It is in the smoky, bustling cafés of Paris that many an irreverent idea emerged, giving birth to a new genre of artists that shunned the old norms of Realism in favor of embracing the freedom of Impressionism.

Opposite: At the Moulin Rouge, *by Henri de Toulouse-Lautrec, was painted between 1892 and 1895. Toulouse-Lautrec himself can be seen in the background, to the left.*

Absinthe Is Mightier Than the Pen

The mists of absinthe curl through the very zeitgeist of Paris's Bohemian Period. The tapestry of colors, the richness of language – the liquor was considered an artistic muse during the decadence that marked the age. From sculpture to paint, and prose to poetry, the creative works of the time bear its unmistakable imprint.

One such poet, Symbolist Charles Baudelaire, became enveloped in the fashionable excesses of intoxicants requisite for a bohemian existence in Paris. And while the city provided a wealth of subject matter for his musings, he scoffed at its culture, referring to it as "a center radiating universal stupidity."

Baudelaire's angst often found him at odds with the public and critics alike. His work, *Les Paradis Artificiels*, disparaged the fake mysticism that was riding a wave of popularity. In an era that Baudelaire viewed as plagued by a desire to seek shortcuts to spiritual enlightenment, he praised drugs and alcohol as the most convenient route to an instant paradise, insisting, "Be drunk always!" The subversive nature of his works drew legal action to suppress what were deemed attacks upon morality. Eventually, he would come to terms with his addictions, noting that he had felt "a breath of wind of the wings of madness." However, he would eventually succumb to the consequences of his indiscretions in 1867 at the age of forty-six.

Poetry through Clouds of Chaos and Passion

Another member of the Symbolist poetical movement was lauded French poet Paul Verlaine. Like Baudelaire, Verlaine applied symbolic meaning to imagery and objects. And like Baudelaire, Verlaine was an absinthe drinker. In 1870, the twenty-six-year-old Verlaine married a young woman about ten years his junior, who became pregnant soon thereafter.

Following two years of marriage, Verlaine's life became unduly complicated when he relinquished regular employment in favor of a career in drinking. It would become only more so upon receiving a letter from a rambunctious young poet named Arthur Rimbaud. A free-spirited youth of sixteen, Rimbaud's poetic genius and disregard for social convention fascinated Verlaine, who introduced him to his circle of bohemian friends and their absinthe-drinking lifestyle. Eventually the two would become lovers, which had the effect of adding even more upheaval to Verlaine's troubled world.

With Verlaine becoming increasingly fixated upon Rimbaud and absinthe, he all but lost interest in his wife and child, whom he physically abused and soon abandoned. Common sense had been replaced by violence and debauchery. To further this trend, Rimbaud's cavalier abandonment of all social convention tested the moral standards of even the most liberal of Verlaine's bohemian associates. Rimbaud's pursuit of perpetual derangement challenged the tolerance of those around him. Rimbaud's recklessness and Verlaine's inability to restrain him became a constant source of turbulence and quarreling.

The two traveled to London in 1872 amidst a cloud of tension, and scratched together an impoverished living. The situation soon became unbearable for Verlaine, who returned to Paris in 1873. Unable to abandon his longing for Rimbaud,

Verlaine traveled to Belgium, inviting Rimbaud to join him. The reunion would reignite the old quarreling, and Verlaine took refuge in drink. Soon thereafter, while in a fit of rage, Verlaine fired a pistol at Rimbaud, which caused a superficial wound.

Above: Henri Thiriet illustrated this richly colored poster for Absinthe Berthelot.

Opposite: Charles Baudelaire (1821–1867), drawn by Henri de Toulouse-Lautrec

Rimbaud handled the incident calmly, but decided to leave. This had the effect of enraging Verlaine, giving Rimbaud sufficient cause to contact the police. An investigation soon revealed the homosexual nature of their relationship, and Verlaine was sentenced to two years in prison. Upon his release, he found himself estranged from his family and friends. Swearing off the evil absinthe, Verlaine soon traveled again to England, where he resumed his life as an educator.

In 1877, Verlaine returned to France, where he became an English teacher in Paris. It is during that time that he met a pupil, Lucien Létinois, who inspired Verlaine to write more poetry. When Létinois suddenly died from typhus in 1883, Verlaine was shattered. In his latter days, he became a destitute alcoholic and addict. He was frequently spotted milling about the cafés of the Quartier Latin in tatters, having become reduced to a rather pathetic muse to a curious public. Verlaine's ragged lifestyle would soon get the better of him, as by his own admission, "For me, my glory is a humble, ephemeral absinthe." He died in 1896, at the age of fifty-one.

Upon his departure from the world of Paul Verlaine, Rimbaud briefly indulged himself in writing, composing several notable works. In 1876, he abandoned writing and joined the Dutch Colonial Army, traveling to the Dutch East Indies. Shortly thereafter, he deserted and returned to France. Rimbaud assumed a life as a trader and merchant, spending most of his time in East Africa. In 1891, he returned to France for treatment for a lesion on his knee. It turned out to be bone cancer. He would die in Marseilles later that year at the age of thirty-seven.

Opposite: Poet Paul Verlaine, painted by Georges Rouault

Left: This Absinthe Terminus poster features two famous stage actors of the day, Constant Coquelin and Sarah Bernhardt.

Below: Featuring the same image as the well-known poster, this Absinthe Terminus tobacco box was a gift for loyal customers.

Oscar Wilde

Perhaps the most famous of Great Britain's absinthe imbibers was a young Irish playwright who was already decorated for his skill in verse even before attending Oxford. A man of physical stature and a flare for style, Oscar Wilde founded the Aesthetic Movement, which promoted the value of purely aesthetic art, literature, and music, sometimes described with the maxim, "Art for art's sake."

Wilde's razor-sharp wit and skill in both written verse and conversation vaulted him into notoriety. He is credited with forging quips such as, "What difference is there between a glass of absinthe and a sunset?" and "Absinthe makes the tart grow fonder." His expertise in Aestheticism earned him an invitation to travel to America on a lecture tour, where he is recorded to have had experiences as diverse as drinking whiskey with miners in Colorado and visiting the Old Absinthe House in the Paris of the New World, New Orleans. Similarly, Wilde enjoyed extensive stays in Paris, where he indulged in the irreverent bohemian culture and his writings, only to return to London upon running out of money. It is during his time in Paris, circa 1882, that one evening at the Café François Premier Wilde was brought vis-à-vis with Paul Verlaine. It was a rather memorable incident, with the flamboyant Wilde being somewhat dumbstruck with pity at the relatively tattered Verlaine. An account of the

Author and critic Oscar Wilde, ca. 1880

meeting noted that Wilde's pleasantries went largely unheeded, as Verlaine kept nodding to his (empty) absinthe glass. Wilde was so distressed by his interaction with Verlaine that he remarked that he could not bear to meet him again.

Wilde was no stranger to the virtues of extended café visits, where he occasionally indulged in the liquid green lubricant. In London, Wilde is known to have been a patron of the famous Café Royal, which remains in operation at its original location at 68 Regent Street in the Piccadilly district. It is in this venue that Wilde is said to have made a fateful decision that would forever change is life.

A man of reasonable means, Wilde had married Constance Lloyd in 1884 with whom he had two children. His interest in his marriage waned after several years, however – particularly upon meeting and beginning an affair with a young Canadian by the name of Robert Ross. Over the course of the next several years, Wilde penned children's books, hit plays, and what became a popular novel. In 1895 Wilde was left a calling card by John Douglas, the Marquess of Queensberry, which bore the accusation, "For Oscar Wilde posing Somdomite [*sic*]," letting Wilde know that the Marquess had become aware of the affair Wilde was having with his son, Lord Alfred Douglas. It was in the Café Royal, under the admonishment of the younger Douglas and against the advice of his friends, that Wilde decided to pursue legal action for libel.

Wilde's fateful decision resulted in damning evidence being brought forth that demonstrated Wilde was a practicing homosexual, which resulted in charges of sodomy and gross indecency, and a subsequent jail term. Following two years of incarceration, Wilde was released and promptly traveled to Naples to meet Douglas before relocating permanently to Paris. Wilde's existence in Paris would be short-lived, as he became critically ill from cerebral meningitis. As Wilde convalesced in a hotel that would be his final stop, his last words are said to be something to the effect of, "This wallpaper and I are fighting a duel to the death. Either it goes or I go." He succumbed to his illness shortly thereafter, dying bankrupt at the age of forty-six.

Oscar Wilde's tomb in the Pere Lachaise Cemetery in Paris, France. It is a tradition for visitors to kiss the tomb while wearing lipstick.

Speaking Truth to Power through the Absurd

The literary world has produced few characters as colorful as Surrealist and Symbolist Alfred Jarry. As a schoolboy, Jarry couldn't help but poke fun at a bumbling teacher, which evolved into a play involving marionettes. The caricatures invoked in this pastime would give birth to one that became the bizarre character known as Ubu, the star of Jarry's most famous work, *Ubu Roi* (1896).

Jarry would soon discover the wonders of absinthe, which he affectionately referred to as the "green goddess." Upon being discharged from the army amidst a gaggle of laughs, Jarry took up residence in Paris, where he indulged in writing clever absurdities. He was viewed as an intelligent, albeit bizarre and unpredictable character, which no doubt caused minor controversy in social settings. Furthermore, given Jarry's disdain for water as a poison (in part because fish urinate in it), he would take his absinthe without it, seemingly confirming the age-old wisdom that only a lunatic would take it neat. Like fellow Symbolists who preceded him, Jarry also adopted the philosophy that intoxication was the path to artistic purity.

The evening of December 10, 1896, saw the opening of his play *Ubu Roi*, the production of which was a feat in itself, given the absurdity of the work. Of particular note was the opening line, *"Merdre!"* – a humorous twist on the expletive *shit*. The effect was a solid fifteen minutes of audience pandemonium – a blend of laughter, cheers, boos, and whistling. Despite an evening of such interruptions, the spectacle vaulted Jarry into fame, something he capitalized on by immersing himself in his absurd world.

Jarry's mockery of Parisian society led him to adopt the absurdities expressed by his fictitious characters, undoubtedly to the annoyance of those he encountered. He was known for pronouncing every silent letter in the French language – with emphasis. He named his bicycle Clément, and carried a loaded pistol. His apartment was configured such that the ceiling was just high enough for his small five-foot stature, which necessitated that his guests stoop or crouch. Perhaps Jarry's most amusing "accomplishment" came through his invention of pataphysics, a pseudoscience of bizarre explanations, in which every event in the universe, no matter how mundane and repeatable, is deemed extraordinary.

Jarry's antics fortified his heroic status among his peers, but his lifestyle of intoxicants, complicated by the ravages of tuberculosis, brought about an early end. His penchant for the absurd was seemingly uninterrupted by the deathbed, where it is said that his last request was, oddly enough, for a toothpick. Jarry died in 1907 at the age of thirty-four.

Opposite: French collectible postcard Une Absinthe Irrésistible depicts rather risqué humor.

Top Right: Cover art for Alfred Jarry's published version of Ubu Roi

Bottom Right: Bottles of older and more recent Spanish absinthes, including Argenti and Pernod Fils Tarragona

Ernest Hemingway

The works of Ernest Hemingway frequently reference absinthe, and it's no surprise that the author was a lifelong aficionado of the drink. From *For Whom the Bell Tolls* to *The Sun Also Rises*, Hemingway's characters frequently turn to and savor absinthe as a drink of choice.

The author likely first encountered absinthe after he relocated to Paris at the admonishment of novelist Sherwood Anderson, who described it as where "the most interesting people in the world live."

His association with Gertrude Stein and acquaintance with famous Parisian writers and artists during his stay in Paris (1921–1928) ensured that he became well versed in the role absinthe played during the Belle Époque – but being born in 1899, he was a bit late to the party. France, however, served as a convenient launching point for excursions into Spain, and it is there that Hemingway cultivated his penchant for the green muse, sipping it with friends in Barcelona, and going so far as to note in his short story *The Strange Country* (1946)

that surviving stocks of pre-ban absinthe in those times were preferable to the contemporary Spanish versions of pre-ban French brands being produced under license.

Upon returning to the Western Hemisphere in 1928, Hemingway relocated to Key West, Florida, during the terrible period known as Prohibition, where he evidently procured bottles of absinthe while on fishing trips to nearby Cuba.

Ernest Hemingway

In a 1931 letter, he remarks,

"Got tight last night on absinthe and did knife tricks. Great success shooting the knife underhand into the piano. The woodworms are so bad and eat hell out of all the furniture that you can always claim the woodworms did it."

Eventually, Hemingway's association with absinthe would be widely known, as an absinthe-laced champagne cocktail from the period was dubbed *Death in the Afternoon*, clearly in homage to his non-fiction account of Spanish bullfighting of the same name, first published in 1932. After a lengthy, distinguished career in writing, Hemingway would take his own life in 1961, following episodes of heavy drinking and depression.

Right: Rare large topettes were commonly used to serve absinthe in a bar. Topettes are a way of measuring multiple doses of absinthe. These bottles have markings etched onto their reverse side, indicating the number of doses.

A Picture Is Worth a Thousand Sips

Until the mid-nineteenth century, the art world was subject to standards of content and style that largely restricted fine art to the subjects of religious events, mythological scenes, and portraits. In France, the Académie des Beaux-Arts upheld these standards, going so far as to scrutinize art based on the attention to finishing details; few observable traces of the artist's individuality, such as brushstrokes or technique, remained. Such was the pattern of Realism, which aimed to depict scenes most objectively, without the influence of supernatural elements or dramatic color.

Édouard Manet hailed from a family of respectable social status, and opened his own Parisian art studio in 1856 following travels around Europe to study various works of art. Having clearly followed the standards of Realism in his earlier days, Manet undertook a deliberate departure from those rules. He favored instead an unorthodox style, one that discarded traditional tones and exhibited an unusual technique in which his brushstrokes remained distinct, infusing his works with an individualistic texture. Such brazen unconventionality simultaneously drew the admiration of young bohemian artists and the criticism of the Académie.

It is the notorious rejection of Manet's *Le Déjeuner sur l'herbe* (*The Luncheon on the Grass*, 1862) that some credit as the launch of the Impressionist age.

The Académie was appalled by Manet's use of vivid colors and "slapdash" brushstrokes – not to mention, the subject matter of a completely nude woman having a picnic luncheon with two fully dressed men seemed contrary to propriety. However, it is his first original and first important work, *Le Buveur d'absinthe* (*The Absinthe Drinker*), from 1859, that showcases Manet's departure from "good taste," which was reinforced upon its rejection that same year from the Salon, the annual exhibition by the Académie des Beaux-Arts.

Manet was known to frequent the popular Tortoni's Café at the time, where his peers included contemporary figures such as fellow artist Gustave Courbet and Baudelaire. Manet and Baudelaire were good friends, which suggests the influence of Baudelaire's *Les Fleurs du mal* in Manet's choice of subject for his painting – a man by the name of Collardet, a beggar who frequented the Louvre.

The rejection of Manet's early works by the Salon was hardly surprising given the relatively subversive nature of these paintings, but this only strengthened his resolve as an artist, giving confirmation to Baudelaire's idea that the confines of societal norms should not deter artists from remaining true to their vision.

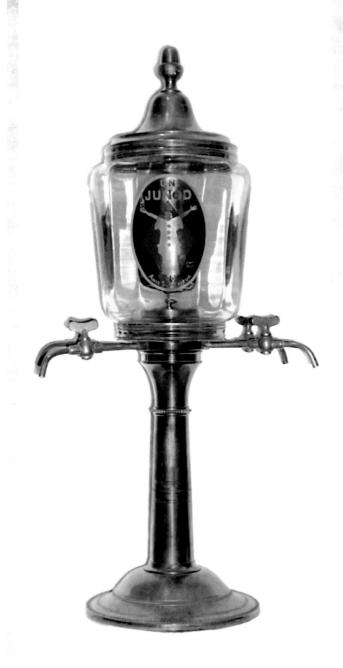

Opposite: The Absinthe Drinker *is thought to be the first major painting, and first original work by Édouard Manet.*

Right: French Junod pastis fountain – this style of both pre-ban and post-ban absinthe fountains persisted in France until the mid-twentieth century.

Green Clouds at the Café

During Manet's time, the burgeoning working-class population in Paris supported a tremendous number of cafés and cabarets, which were well versed in serving absinthe to thirsty patrons. Some of these venues, such as the Moulin Rouge in the red-light district of Pigalle, became globally renowned for their artistic, risqué revelry. They were frequented by colorful characters such as Henri de Toulouse-Lautrec, Vincent van Gogh, and Paul Gauguin. But of all the cafés and bistros in the city, perhaps none were as familiar with *L'Heure Verte*, or the Green Hour, as those in the Montmartre area, which served as the epicenter around which the bohemian writers and artists revolved.

One such popular café was the Nouvelle-Athènes at Place Pigalle. In 1876, this café served as the backdrop from which Edgar Degas would create his famous painting *L'Absinthe* (*The Absinthe Drinker*) – with his acquaintances, fellow artist Marcellin Desboutin and actress Ellen Andrée – serving as its subjects. The pair is depicted sitting at a marble table, with Desboutin drinking what appears to be an innocuous coffee while smoking a pipe. Sitting next to him in an apparent stupor and seemingly oblivious to her surroundings is Andrée, and placed before her on the table is a glass of cloudy green liquid that is unmistakably absinthe.

Degas's painting caused quite a stir, with Andrée being chastised in particular for her role in allowing Degas to create such a monstrosity. The criticism was so severe, in fact, that the painting was put into storage, not being shown again until it was taken to England in 1893. London Victorian society considered the painting an abomination of morality, and it stoked feelings of Francophobia. Additionally, the work was perceived to be a warning against the consumption of absinthe and the degradation to propriety it caused. The painting was eventually sold to a British collector, and survives today as a classic example of Impressionist art.

Above: Absinthe Drinker *(also known as* L'Absinthe *and* Glass of Absinthe*) was painted by Edgar Degas in 1876.*

Opposite: The original Moulin Rouge burned down in 1915. It featured a red windmill on its roof, and is considered the birthplace of the cancan dance.

The Condition of van Gogh

Perhaps none of the absinthe-quaffing artists of the period was as famous and controversial as Vincent van Gogh. While his problems began well in advance of his arrival in Paris in the spring of 1886, van Gogh no doubt found Paris to be welcoming of his habits of drinking and smoking in excess. Some claim that it was the two artists he befriended, Henri de Toulouse-Lautrec and Paul Gauguin, who introduced him to absinthe and prostitutes, but it is quite likely that he would have found them anyway. Having completed more than two hundred paintings in two years' time, van Gogh found himself exhausted by Paris, and moved to Arles in the south of France.

Despite dealing with chronic illnesses as a result of his smoking and absinthe drinking, van Gogh intended to establish a utopian art colony in Arles. Eventually, he convinced his Parisian acquaintance Gauguin to visit in Arles, and the two shared a house. After a couple of months, Gauguin grew increasingly intolerant of van Gogh, who similarly resented Gauguin's superior attitude. The two quarreled about art, and there was an air of constant tension. The situation reached a crisis point upon Gauguin announcing his departure, which triggered van Gogh to make physical threats, culminating in the famous self-mutilation incident in

Left: Vincent van Gogh painted this self-portrait in 1889, while in asylum at St.-Remy, where he committed himself following a mental breakdown.

Opposite: Farmhouse in Provence, *by van Gogh, 1888, painted during the artist's productive stay in Arles*

which he severed part of his ear, almost bleeding to death as a result.

Theories abound as to the causes of van Gogh's mania, but it seems clear that he suffered from a host of psychiatric disorders and possibly syphilis, all of which were undoubtedly exacerbated by his substance abuse and weak physical condition. He checked himself into a mental hospital in May 1889, the remainder of his short life mottled with numerous paintings in between psychotic episodes. It was during these experiences that the artist was said to have resorted to such habits as drinking turpentine and ingesting paints. It is also claimed that he continued drinking absinthe during this time, often being gifted bottles from well-wishing friends. The constant cloud of depression eventually became too much for van Gogh to endure, and he shot himself in July 1890. And while van Gogh managed to sell merely one painting in his entire lifetime, his works are now priceless.

Toulouse-Lautrec: Absinthe's Favored Son

One individual van Gogh befriended while in Paris was an eccentric character of relatively diminished physical stature by the name of Henri de Toulouse-Lautrec. Having originated from an aristocratic family that was subject to inbreeding – his own parents were first cousins – Lautrec suffered congenital issues as a child, most notably resulting in stunted growth after breaking both femurs when he was an adolescent. While his upper body was normally proportioned, his legs ceased growing and his mature height barely reached five feet as a result. Being unable to participate in physical activities, the young Lautrec took a keen interest in art, for which he displayed considerable talent. By the age of eighteen, he was sent by his mother to study with the masters in Paris. While being formally schooled in the finer points of classical art, Lautrec soon abandoned that direction in favor of Impressionism.

Lautrec became an inhabitant of the bohemian center of Montmarte, where he resided for some twenty years. It is there, amidst the avant-garde revelry of this bohemian center, that Lautrec developed his niche for portraying taboo subjects, such as workers in the sex industry, in a manner that was deemed sensible and humane. Lautrec's paintings were the subject of art exhibitions and open-air displays, both of which earned him considerable notoriety and secured much commissioned work. One

distinguishing element of Lautrec's style was derived from his interest in Japanese woodblock prints – an influence evident in many of his commissioned posters. The proceeds from such work earned Lautrec a reasonable living. Also, being a reasonably good English speaker, Lautrec traveled to London, where he befriended Oscar Wilde, and engaged in additional commissioned advertisements.

When the Moulin Rouge opened nearby in 1889, Lautrec was commissioned to create a series of posters for the now famous venue. Befittingly, the Moulin Rouge always reserved a seat for Lautrec, who was a regular patron and befriended the performers, many of whom appeared in his paintings. Lautrec also frequented other cabarets, brothels, dance halls, and bars of Montmartre, all of which profoundly impacted his continuous stream of ideas, which he would sketch by night and paint by day. Being viewed somewhat as a physical outlier, it is no surprise that Lautrec often hired the services of prostitutes. He empathized with them as sharing a similar dilemma: he was excluded from society because of his physical condition, they because of their moral transgressions.

Lautrec's limited physical stature did nothing to limit his propensity to drink, which was hardly considered inappropriate in the parlors of excess that he favored. Lautrec found a friend in absinthe, and to ensure he was never without it, he sported a hollow walking stick that was filled with the liquid green elixir. He is noted for louching his absinthe with not water but cognac, the resulting mix being referred to as a *Tremblement de Terre* (Earthquake).

Above: La Goulue, *painted by Henri de Toulouse-Lautrec in 1891, was used as an advertising poster for the French club Moulin Rouge. It shows the famous cancan dancer La Goulue and her flexible partner, Valentine le Désossé.*

Opposite: Self-portrait of Henri de Toulouse-Lautrec

Lautrec expressed other ideas in the creative mixing of absinthe, also louching it with red or white wine in artfully layered cocktails he called "Rainbow Cups."

Lautrec's philosophy of "drink little, but drink often," eventually overcame his constitution, causing him to collapse from exhaustion and chronic alcoholism. He was committed to a sanatorium for three months in 1899, where his recovery resulted in thirty-nine circus-performer portraits. Upon his release, he returned to Paris briefly, and then departed his city studio to travel around France. Eventually, alcoholism and syphilis, the latter of which he contracted from a prostitute, caught up with him. He died of complications from his indiscretions in 1901, at the age of thirty-six.

Mists of Green through the Blue Period

Paris became home to another of the most influential figures of Belle Époque art, the inimitable Pablo Picasso. A native of Andalusia, Picasso moved to Paris at the age of twenty in 1901 to further his art skills. Devastated by the suicide of his friend Carlos Casagemas, Picasso's "Blue Period" spawned dark works that illustrated beggars, prostitutes, and addicts – the seedy underbelly of Parisian society. Picasso traveled back and forth between Paris and Barcelona, collecting impressions of the darker elements of bohemian life from both of these vibrant cities. While not noted to be a habitual absinthe fancier himself, Picasso bore witness to scenes of nocturnal absinthe drinkers, and immortalized several stunning works in gothic palettes that depict what are oftentimes gaunt and ghastly characters indulging in the green liquid. Picasso's perspective from his subjects appears to be one of a voyeur, likely

in part due to his apparent restraint from allowing himself to become engulfed in the common intoxicants of the era. Furthermore, Picasso was able to attract buyers for his works of art, which endowed him with some fame and finances from a relatively early age. It is almost certainly Picasso's discretion as a young man that afforded him a lifespan well beyond those of many of his less fortunate contemporaries.

Curiously enough, many of the artistic works of the Belle Époque would go largely unappreciated in their time. Those who broke the rules followed by their masters and mentors did so because they rejected the conventions of the bourgeoisie in favor of the freedom to enjoy each passing moment, as opposed to structuring their lives around a predetermined path toward eventual wealth and delayed gratification. Absinthe served as a liquid catalyst for these ideas, and the sheer popularity of the green spirit earned it its place as an icon of freedom – a ticket into a carefree world of unregulated intoxication, revelry, and promiscuity. This era would come to an abrupt end at the onset of the First World War, which carved a path of destruction through the heart of the French nation.

Above: A rare postcard depicts a temptress who simultaneously displays the vices of smoking, sex, and drinking absinthe

Opposite: Pablo Picasso: Self-Portrait *(1901)*

2

The
Ascension and Demise
of the
GREEN FAIRY

To fully gauge absinthe's impact on the literary and art world, it helps to understand the drink's long and storied history. Well before the distilled spirit rose to prominence as a fashionable drink with a curious reputation, the ancients noted the medicinal attributes of its namesake herb in early pharmacopeia.

The ancient Egyptians were believed to have combined a plant called absinthium, often referred to as "grand wormwood," with other regional ingredients, such as juniper berries, fennel, honey, and wine or beer, to create a beverage believed to have medicinal power. Such absinthium-laced potions were prescribed for various digestive ailments, fevers, menstrual complaints, and other common maladies.

Across the Mediterranean, in the civilizations of ancient Greece and Rome, absinthium was claimed to be a vermifuge and general digestive aid, as well as an abortifacient, remedy for jaundice, and treatment for bad breath.

Absinthium continued to be recognized for its value in treating digestive complaints in both man and beast through the Middle Ages and into the Renaissance, although the centuries-old practice of mulling its foliage in beer or wine invariably resulted in a terribly bitter concoction that was unpalatable by all accounts.

The intense bitterness of the herb is perhaps why the people of seventeenth-century England popularized purl, an ale seasoned with a less bitter cousin,

Opposite: One of the most widely recognized absinthe posters, Absinthe Bourgeois (1902) was created by the Mourgue brothers during the height of the absinthe craze.

Wormwood

"Wormwood" is a nickname that is casually applied to any of several hundred species of plants in the *Artemisia* genus, all of which belong to the daisy family (*Asteraceae*). This genus includes notable botanicals of culinary and medicinal value such as tarragon (*Artemisia dracunculus*), mugwort (*Artemisia vulgaris*), sweet annie (*Artemisia annua*), and many others.

Of these, one particular perennial species grows up to two meters (six feet) in height, with silvery green foliage, yellow button-like inflorescence, a heady minty aroma, and an intensely bitter flavor. This is *Artemisia absinthium*, aka "grand absinthe" or "grand wormwood," the namesake herb of the famous spirit, as well as its most essential ingredient.

Artemisia maritima, that was popular with the working class and served in many a bawdy house. Undoubtedly, it is the reason why in his period work *The Complete* *Herbal* (1653), Nicholas Culpeper describes distilling absinthium with "annis" seeds, which would have neutralized the herb's powerfully unpleasant flavor.

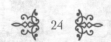

The Birth of a Spirit

Legend has it that Pierre Ordinaire, a French doctor who lived just across the border in Switzerland, invented the basis of what would become modern absinthe toward the end of the eighteenth century. Upon taking up residence in the scenic Val-de-Travers region of that country, Ordinaire experimented with the art of distillation, using both native and exotic flora that were renowned for their medicinal virtues. And while no one can claim with certainty that Ordinaire invented the concept of distilling absinthe with flavorful seeds (as Culpeper described more than a century before), Ordinaire is credited with creating a noteworthy distilled digestive tonic from grand absinthe, green anise (*Pimpinella anisum*), and sweet fennel (*Foeniculum vulgare*), along with others such as hyssop (*Hyssopus officinalis*), lemon balm (*Melissa officinalis*), and petite absinthe (*Artemisia pontica*).

Ordinaire's creation had several distinct benefits over any similar concoction that had come before. First, the distillation resolved the bitterness problem

Maison PERNOD Fils
10. - Sortie du Personnel

By the time Henri-Louis Pernod died in December 1851, his once-humble distillery had grown into a large building on the banks of the Doubs River.

by drawing out and condensing the medicinal essences of the herb, while joining the distillate with the pleasant flavor of two "hot seeds." Then, he gave the resulting medicine a post-distillation infusion of botanicals that had a delicate aroma and flavor. These latter botanicals also provided the pleasant natural olive tint. The result was a proprietary digestive tonic that was as delicious as it was potent. Ordinaire graciously shared the fruits of his labor with patients and guests, who marveled at the powers of this "wonder drug."

Lore has it that before his death, Ordinaire disclosed the recipe for his herbal potion to the two Henriod sisters of Couvet, Switzerland, who continued to prepare Ordinaire's creation to the delight of traveling guests. It was one such guest, Major Daniel-Henri Dubied, who recognized the economic potential of a liquid so magical it could be a balm for all digestive complaints. In a stroke of entrepreneurship, Dubied purchased the recipe from the Henriod sisters and began distilling the medicine locally in Couvet in 1797. Enlisting the aid of his son Marcelin and his son-in-law Henri-Louis Perrenoud, Dubied capitalized on his son-in-law's distilling knowledge to launch a modest operation that he called Dubied Père et Fils.

By 1805, with most clientele being drawn from the French side of the border, and given the high taxes associated with exporting the Swiss spirit,

Left: The French artist and illustrator Alexandre Graverol (1865–1949) was well acquainted with absinthe. His delicate watercolors evoke the magic and mystery of absinthe and here incorporates a floating head of Paul Verlaine, a glass of absinthe, opium poppies, and occultist imagery.

Henri-Louis, who had changed the spelling of his last name to "Pernod," reestablished the distillery in the French border town of Pontarlier. He constructed the distillery, consisting of two stills producing around sixteen liters each per day, in a small rented house. Little did Henri-Louis realize what the future had in store for his sleepy regional elixir.

Medicine for the Masses

At the advent of the nineteenth century, France was on a fast track of cultural and technological change.

Old ideas gave way to the new, and Europe flourished in the blossoming of the Industrial Age. With advances in technology came advances in communication and transportation, such as the convenience of rail travel, which put all parts of the nation within easy reach.

Meanwhile, advances in agricultural technology gave rise to large-scale farming, which pushed the rural poor to urban centers such as Paris and Lyon in search of service-industry jobs. Much of this work involved difficult physical labor, long hours, and low wages. Nonetheless, by the mid-nineteenth century, the population of Paris alone had swelled to around double its pre-Revolution figure.

In Times of War

During the Algerian Campaign (1844–1847), France seized control of Algeria from the Ottoman Empire. This campaign presented numerous challenges to the young men of the French army, as they wrestled with the hostile terrain and climate of North Africa, as well as sanitation issues that invariably led to illness.

As part of its guarantee to provide clean drinking water, the army issued its soldiers rations of absinthe, as the spirit's powers of disinfection were purportedly able to render potentially unclean water *hygiénique*. Perhaps French soldiers discovered a preference for adding a little water to absinthe as opposed to the other way around, but abuse of the delicious anise-flavored medicine soon became rampant. The soldiers' glaring taste for absinthe achieved considerable publicity back in France, as humorous sketches mocking the "absinthe military" began appearing in popular journals.

When the soldiers returned to France and stepped back into their civilian lives, they retained their taste for the curiously potent anise-flavored medicine that they had befriended in the desert and within the cafés of Algeria. This brought the spirit from its origins as a regional delicacy into the mainstream of urban culture.

The Rise of Café Culture

The Industrial Revolution also brought demographic shifts that changed the very face of Europe. With the population boom in urban areas came a swelling in numbers of young people, many of whom found difficulty securing steady work. Marginalized to the fringe of society, many of these younger people rejected and ridiculed the bourgeois ideals upon which they were reared. The counterculture they spawned embraced a rejection of conventional societal structure and material wealth in favor of expressing contrarian ideas, all while embracing a lifestyle rife with intoxicating spirits, drugs, and promiscuous sexual freedom. Much like the hippie movement of the 1960s, their carefree behavior and nomad-like mobility were compared with that of the notorious Romani people of the day, who were associated with a region of the Czech Republic known as Bohemia. As such, this new class of citizens became whimsically referred to as bohemians.

The lifestyle of a French bohemian was one that often involved eating little while drinking and smoking in excess. And because the bohemian movement thrived on social exchanges, urban cafés served as congregational centers for the bohemian set, which regularly migrated from one café to another as the evening wore into the late hours.

Café Procope was one such café that witnessed many an inebriated but intellectual debate among famous bohemian habitués, and it is often considered to be the oldest Parisian restaurant in continuous operation, since its debut in 1686. It remains in good order today at its original location at Rue de l'Ancienne Comédie, adjacent to the lively Boulevard Saint-Germain, which is historically renowned for its cafés.

The bohemians befriended absinthe rather early in its rise to popularity, marveling at its preparation ritual, flavor, color, and potency. And as absinthe became the fashionable tipple during the early evening hours when aperitifs are appropriate, that time became known as *L'Heure Verte*, or the Green Hour, in homage to the delectable spirit.

Burning Down the House of Pernod

As the dawn of the twentieth century arrived, absinthe was big business. Having long since outgrown its days as a regional liquor in sleepy Franco-Swiss villages, absinthe had become recognized not only as the national drink of France but also as an object of global commerce. This was in part due to the popularity of intoxicating spirits booming throughout Europe, but it was also a result of the epidemic of phylloxera – a plant louse that crippled continental vineyards toward the end of the nineteenth century.

Then on August 11, 1901, a fire raged out of control at the distillery of Pernod Fils in Pontarlier, the largest absinthe producer in France – or the world, for that matter. To lessen the degree of devastation, huge vats of absinthe were opened and drained into the Doubs River; its waters soon turned milky white and smelled strongly of absinthe. The fire was hot enough to melt glass, and continued smoldering for four days.

Down but not out, the Pernod Fils distillery was promptly reconstructed with the intention of becoming the most modern distillery in the world, flaunting the very best technological wizardry available. By 1908, Henri-Louis's namesake distillery was producing more than 20,000 liters of absinthe per day, totaling more than five million liters a year.

Above: A stack of these original labels was found in an old distillery in Couvet, Switzerland. These labels were affixed to the back of bottles of Edouard Pernod absinthe bound for export.

Left: Pernod Fils put out a series of postcards depicting the various aspects of the distillery; this one highlights workers in the bottling section of the factory.

Opposite: The famous Procope Café in Paris, once a favorite haunt of absinthe drinkers. Opened in 1686, it is the longest continuously operating café in France.

Above: This postcard depicts infants enjoying absinthe at six p.m. – l'Heure Verte.

Opposite: Famous occultist Aleister Crowley

Meanwhile, across the English Channel

While the popularity of absinthe swept across France, the controversy surrounding the drink and the thoroughly publicized decadence of the culture with which it was associated caused it to have a somewhat tempered reception in Victorian England. However, while the British remained steadfast in their general preference for frothy ales, Old Tom gin, and whiskey, the fashionably hip were well versed in the virtues of the green French spirit that permeated the artistic circles of London.

Around the time that Oscar Wilde succumbed to meningitis, Englishman Edward Alexander Crowley was twenty-five years of age, residing in London, and actively practicing magic with the cultish Hermetic Order of the Golden Dawn.

Crowley was born in 1875 to wealthy Christian fundamentalists. Having never formed a good relationship with his mother, Crowley's life was upended at the age of eleven when he lost his father to cancer. Crowley was no stranger to committing rebellious acts out of spite over his strict Christian upbringing, and unhappy with his given names, Crowley changed his first name to Aleister.

Despite having spent several years at Cambridge, Crowley departed without achieving a degree, whereupon he became fully engaged in his practice of the occult with the Golden Dawn. Crowley frequently found himself at odds with more esteemed members of the group, which included figures such as William Butler Yeats, Sir Arthur Conan Doyle, Maud Gonne, Arthur Machen, Arthur Edward Waite, Florence Farr, and Algernon Blackwood, as well as (reputedly) Sax Rohmer and Bram Stoker.

Having fallen into disfavor with the group, Crowley relocated to Mexico for a while, subsequently embarking upon a series of worldwide travels that provided a constantly changing backdrop for his studies in the occult and mysticism. His travels eventually landed him in Paris, where he married self-proclaimed clairvoyant Rose Kelly. The two then relocated to Cairo, and Crowley experienced what he claimed to be a profound spiritual breakthrough. The next several years of his life involved a whirlwind of travel to various countries, the writing of various occultist works, and engaging in the art of magic, which involved mysticism, drugs, and sex acts. Ironically, Crowley then divorced his wife because of her alcoholism.

By the outbreak of World War I, Crowley, who was struggling financially, relocated to the United States, where he worked secretly as a British agent. In 1916, Crowley moved again, this time to New Orleans. He became a regular visitor to the Old Absinthe House, where he wrote his famous sonnet *Absinthe: The Green Goddess*, while awaiting a lady friend in a dimly lit corner of the bar that he proclaimed to be "the heart and soul of the old quarter." In his timeless ode to the seductive green spirit, Crowley quips, "It is as if the first diviner of absinthe had been indeed a magician intent upon a combination of sacred drugs [botanicals] which should cleanse, fortify and perfume the human soul."

Following the war, Crowley returned to London and wrote *Diary of a Drug Fiend*, which caused alarm in the press. In the years that followed, his antics began wearing thin with publishers and the public alike. Following two world wars and several lifetimes of travel, Crowley found few willing to publish his works, and he became hopelessly addicted to heroin and cocaine. Crowley died a destitute man in 1947 at the age of seventy-two.

During the era when Wilde and Crowley made their marks upon the world, absinthe persisted in England as a French curiosity, but the spirit never reached the height of popularity it enjoyed in France. Perhaps it is due to the more reserved Victorians' Francophobia, but more likely it was because in the British Empire absinthe was more commonly considered a cocktail ingredient, which meant it drew less ire as a destroyer of civilized society – an honor traditionally granted to bad gin.

Absinthe Invades the United States

As the absinthe phenomenon gained steam across the European continent, the Atlantic Ocean proved to be no barrier. In the young American nation, importers of French goods in the relatively cosmopolitan port cities became acquainted with absinthe, as it took its place among fine French brandies and liqueurs.

Absinthe undoubtedly made its most indelible impression in the cosmopolitan melting pot of New Orleans. Founded on the banks of the Mississippi by French explorers, New Orleans provided both a deep-water port and a place of settlement that was thoroughly insulated from the relatively puritanical

Left: Jean Béraud, a French impressionist painter and commercial artist, painted many scenes of nineteenth-century Parisian life. In this image, an elegant patron gently louches a glass of absinthe.

Opposite: The Old Absinthe House's motto is "Everyone you have known or ever will know, eventually ends up at the Old Absinthe House."

mentality that prevailed in the English colonies. New Orleans quickly became the jewel of the agrarian south, providing an attractive escape for continental Europeans wishing to start anew. The relatively tolerant society of New Orleans and the surrounding areas became a safe haven for the historically oppressed.

In keeping close its French influences and largely French-speaking population, New Orleans was awash in all things *Français*. As the largest southern city until around 1900, the volume of international and domestic trade traversing New Orleans ensured it was one of diversity and decadence. It was well known for its virtues in wine, women, gambling, and opportunity.

By 1840, New Orleans importers of French goods were already advertising "absynthe" within their bills of commodities. The spirit was graciously accepted in the "Crescent City," which gradually adopted it into its culture. Nowhere was this more evident than in a coffeehouse located on the corner of Bourbon and Bienville that was reworked in 1874 by a Catalan bartender named Cayetano Ferrér. Having previously served drinks at the basement bar of the nearby French Opera House, Ferrér was already well acquainted with the demand for absinthe. In

fitting acknowledgment of this trend, Ferrér named his new bar the Absinthe Room. By 1890, following sixteen years of success, Ferrér renamed his thriving bar the Old Absinthe House. This icon of the French Quarter had the privilege of serving notable figures such as Mark Twain, Walt Whitman, Oscar Wilde, and the inimitable Aleister Crowley.

The Old Absinthe House distinguished itself by providing absinthe in the traditional French service, via the use of ornate green-and-white marble fountains adorned with Napoleonic bronze statuettes. These fountains were undoubtedly crafted in France, and very possibly served as water fountains in the French Opera House prior to its renovation. Pressed into service as marvelous absinthe fountains, the heavy brass spigots were plumbed via copper pipes to large cypress rainwater cisterns situated on the roof of the building. These fountains remain on location to this very day in the Old Absinthe House, and are perhaps the only surviving, indelible evidence of absinthe being served French-style on American shores.

The popularity of absinthe wasn't limited to New Orleans. By the late nineteenth century, absinthe had found its way to bars and coffeehouses in every major port city and across the interior of the nation. The green French potion had traveled all the way to the West Coast, and even the frontier that was the Pacific Northwest. There, it was

Left: A rare blue-ink etched Absinthe Bourgeois water carafe, now cloudy with calcification from years of use.

Opposite: This advertising poster for Absinthe Duchesse features an innocent and wistful woman.

lyrics making no reservations in waxing poetic over the virtues of the frosty beverage as a most effective antidepressant when all seems lost:

When life seems grey and dark the dawn,
and you are through,
There is, they say, on such a morn, one thing to do:
Rise up and ring, a bell-boy call to you straight-way,
And bid him bring a cold and tall absinthe frappé!

It will free you first from the burning thirst
That is born of a night of the bowl,
Like a sun 'twill rise through the inky skies
That so heavily hang o'er your soul.
At the first cool sip on your fevered lip
You determine to live through the day,
Life's again worthwhile as with a dawning smile
You imbibe your absinthe frappé!

The deed is done so waste no woe o'er yestereen.
Nor swear to shun a year or so the festive scene.
Remorse will pass, despair will fade with speed away
Before a glass of rightly-made absinthe frappé!

It will free you first from the burning thirst
That is born of a night of the bowl,
Like a sun 'twill rise through the inky skies
That so heavily hang o'er your soul.
At the first cool sip on your fevered lip
You determine to live through the day,
Life's again worthwhile as with a dawning smile
You imbibe your absinthe frappé!

It Happened in Nordland

Absinthe also found its way into song, most notably in a Victor Herbert operetta from 1904 entitled *It Happened in Nordland*. The score contained the Glen MacDonough composition "Absinthe Frappé," in homage to a refreshingly potent cocktail appreciated throughout the American nation. This popular tune was impressed upon early Edison cylinders, its

found to be unconventionally useful, as accounted by a Yakima, Washington, newspaper from 1896: "Pour a few drops of absinthe on my fingers," said he. The barkeep did so, and the gentleman rubbed it vigorously into his mustache. "I am going to call on some ladies," he explained, "and want to take the whisky odor away."

Spain

Absinthe was also tippled in the Iberian Peninsula, although it never achieved the same popularity it enjoyed in France and Switzerland. And while the close proximity of Spain and Portugal to France made cultural exchange inevitable, the Iberians never relinquished their preference for sherry, port, and wine in favor of the green import.

Absinthe did find its way into the cafés of the El Raval district of Barcelona, which sported its own bohemian culture. Bar Marsella, the city's oldest drink seller, was known to provide quantities of the seductive liquid to its eccentric clientele. Being a rather avant-garde establishment, Bar Marsella also had its own transvestite theater.

Despite absinthe's moderate presence in Spanish culture, numerous distilleries provided their own versions of the potent liquid, including Destilerías Marí Mayans, founded in 1880 by Juan Mayans, a master of aromatic and medicinal botanicals. Spain probably distilled the most absinthe following the Swiss and French bans of 1910 and 1915, respectively, when Spanish distillers gladly produced licensed

Above: A modern postcard showing a narrow street in Barcelona's Gothic Quarter, where absinthe bars were originally located. Some have remained in business since absinthe's heyday.

Left: Miniature Spanish absinthe bottles

Opposite: This postcard was one of a series of six that showed babies drinking absinthe.

versions of the now-banned Franco-Swiss absinthes. This greatly delighted visitors to the country, whose once abundant sources of pre-ban absinthes were depleted.

The Beginning of the End

Although the booming popularity of absinthe was showing no signs of dimming at the conclusion of the nineteenth century, the phenomenon was certainly not without its consequences. Among these were the mental and physical issues associated with alcoholism, which had become rampant. Urban centers such as Paris and Lyon were awash in drink sellers, with no shortage of regular patrons to support them.

This growing problem gave cause for the medical establishment to invest considerable effort in understanding the effects of alcoholism, which was deemed a mental illness. Many alcoholics were subjected to hydrotherapy treatment – a daily five-hour session of being doused with cold water. Following this, they were discharged as cured of alcoholism, and given strict instructions to restrict their alcohol intake to wine, which was deemed healthy.

Dr. Valentin Jacques Joseph Magnan was a French psychiatrist at the asylum of Sainte-Anne in Paris. Among Dr. Magnan's keen observations, which began in the 1850s, was the startling realization that many who were admitted into the asylum were not only alcoholics, but admitted absinthe drinkers. Having conducted his own studies into

the matter, Magnan concluded that the effects of absinthe abuse were distinctly different from that of common alcoholism, so much so that he coined the term *absinthism*. Magnan went on to claim that abuse of absinthe not only resulted in epilepsy and insanity, but also caused birth defects that could be passed

3. ~ Comme Grand-Père

Lire, c'est pas amusant,
Pour les bébés ; je préfère
Dans le verre de grand-père
Boire un Pernod épatant !

down to several subsequent generations. Magnan's studies were hardly scientific by modern standards, and often involved injecting animals with oil of absinthium, which resulted in erroneous assumptions and misleading conclusions. Nonetheless, his views were enormously influential, and were constantly cited by the temperance movement in their opposition to what had become the national drink.

Magnan wasn't alone in observing the madness. In 1860, journalist and playwright Henri Balesta published a book entitled *Absinthe et absintheurs*. Balesta's book followed the lives of chronic absinthe drinkers, giving special attention to the destructive effects the behavior levied upon the abusers, their families, and the community. Balesta's book provided ample fodder in the effort to blame absinthe for societal ills.

Although at the time it was noted less frequently, it is important to remember that by 1860, the opium trade had all but guaranteed a steady supply of laudanum, morphine, and eventually heroin to abusers. Opiate abuse was common enough that it became acceptable to partake of it in social situations, and gold syringes were crafted as personal accessories.

Similarly, Mariani wine – a Bordeaux wine containing coca leaf extract that created an invigorating drink to combat fatigue – was endorsed by none other than his holiness the pope. It inspired the cocaine- and caffeine-laced temperance tonic that would become the original Coca-Cola. But in the argument against absinthe, the popularity and easy availability of intoxicants such as opiates, cocaine, cannabis, and even ether were often casually overlooked. Compared to these, absinthe was simply "the paregoric of second childhood," according to noted nineteenth-century British actor Maurice Barrymore.

Bad Medicine

"Absinthes are obtained in two ways: by distillation and by essences; the last is always of inferior quality, disastrous for the physiology... It is hardly ever used except in low-class establishments..."

– *Le Liquoriste moderne*, A. Bedel, 1899, France

When any commodity becomes popular, in its wake comes a financially motivated drive to make it cheaper. Absinthe was not spared the effects of such profiteering. Whereas distilling a genuine absinthe demands tremendous volumes of botanicals, expensive equipment, energy, labor, and time, copycat products appeared that were concocted in the warehouses of Paris and Lyon. These knockoff liquors were not produced using traditional methods but rather used cheap industrial alcohols, commercial flavorings, and artificial adulterants – the adverse health effects of all notwithstanding. Unlike the majority of established agricultural commodities of the time, absinthe was protected by neither an appellation nor legal definition.

Additionally, *caveat emptor* was the rule in these times, as the advent of modern food and beverage regulations was decades away. This allowed anything to be bottled and sold as absinthe, and predictably, many cheap, inferior versions of the drink appeared, most often being sold to poor alcoholics. At least some of these cheap absinthes were reputed to leave one with a metallic taste in one's mouth, likely from the artificial colorant copper sulfate, or antimony trichloride, sometimes included to enhance the clouding effect (louche) that consumers demanded.

Opposite: Heures de loisirs aux Colonies – *a postcard depicting a French colonialist in Tahiti in the early 1900s. He is languidly enjoying his hobbies of relaxation and absinthe.*

Left: Alexandre Graverol's fin de siècle watercolor portrays Paul Verlaine in the hospital surrounded by mystical imagery and the omnipresent glass of absinthe at lower left, opposite the holy chalice on the right.

The most commonly used adulterant, commercial oil of wormwood, is a poisonous substance that was used as a flavoring by producers of cheap, inferior absinthes, and was even imported from as far away as the United States for this purpose.

The detrimental impact of these cheap, adulterated absinthes did not go unnoticed by the discriminating public. Many who drank absinthe were inclined to be particularly brand conscious when ordering the drink. The best-selling brand, Pernod Fils, had arisen as a national icon and standard-bearer of the category, much as Coca-Cola is in the realm of soft drinks. Similarly, this had many ordering an absinthe by simply asking for *un Pernod*. Being acutely aware of this brand consciousness, the copycats did not sit idle. Numerous cleverly named knockoff brands appeared, poised to take advantage of Pernod Fils' success. These sported branding such as Parrott and Pierrot, undoubtedly with the intention of deceiving consumers. The proliferation of copycats and inferior brands prompted Pernod Fils to engage in numerous legal battles in an attempt to stem the tide of cheap imposters.

By 1880, the detrimental toll the work of profiteers was taking upon its unwitting victims was a phenomenon known throughout French society. A café patron could order an absinthe simply by asking for *une correspondence*, or "a transfer," referring to a connecting train ticket to Charenton – a well-known insane asylum in the Parisian suburbs.

Sour Grapes

There was a longstanding belief among the French that there were two types of alcohol, the "good" and the "bad." The "good alcohol" consisted of that derived from wine, pears, apples, and beer, all of which were deemed wholesome. Conversely, "bad alcohol" was that created from the distillation of grain and sugar beets.

Being traditionally distilled from *eau-de-vie* of wine, absinthe therefore fell into the category of "good alcohol," which was exploited to great effect in advertisements claiming health benefits from its regular consumption. The concept of "good alcohol" and "bad alcohol" seems absurd from a contemporary viewpoint, but it probably evolved around the limitations of the pot-still technology that prevailed during the first half of the nineteenth century. In 1830, Irishman Aeneas Coffey earned a patent for his novel column still, which proved to be a game changer for the distillation of alcohol. Coffey's efficient column could distill virtually any fermentable material into high purity (i.e., 95% ABV, or alcohol by volume) potable ethanol, and eventually proved to be of great significance in absinthe's epic story.

CEUX QUI BOIVENT

de l'Absinthe

Opposite: Pernod Fils, like other distilleries, incorporated animals such as pigs, monkeys, dogs, and even cats into advertisements, which were whimsically portrayed as dedicated absinthe drinkers.

Right: A tastefully dressed pig represents "those who drink."

In the 1850s, Victorian botanists from England collected specimens of native American grapes. Unbeknownst to them, these vines harbored phylloxera – a louse to which the American vines were impervious, but not the European *Vitis vinifera*. This resulted in an infestation that devastated English vineyards. By the 1870s and 1880s, continental Europe had become infected, which subsequently ravaged the vineyards of France. The aphid-like insect created considerable damage to the wine industry, which caused a significant jump in the price of wine due to its sudden scarcity. The production of French wines was reduced to 10 percent to 30 percent of the normal volume.

This effectively rendered what had always been a common beverage unaffordable to many of the working class. Devastating the brandy industry as well, the phylloxera epidemic also threatened the better absinthe producers, who depended upon a steady supply of wine alcohol for their distillations. Fortunately, the popularity of Coffey's "patent still" during the mid- and latter part of the nineteenth century created an alternate option for absinthe distillers during the phylloxera problem, as they were able to switch to grain or sugar beet alcohol, and undoubtedly many quietly did.

When the wine industry began to recover, absinthe had already supplanted wine as the national drink of France. Not only had the wine industry lost substantial market share, but it had lost the business of selling distilled wine to absinthe producers. Absinthe had become the enemy. By 1900, probably 95 percent (or more) of the world's absinthe originated from distilleries located in the sleepy rural hills along the Franco-Swiss frontier. The French border town of Pontarlier had a population of fewer than ten thousand inhabitants, but was home to twenty-one absinthe distilleries, and absinthe production was at an all-time high.

Above: This temperance poster by Gantner (1910) was originally published in the Swiss satirical publication Le Guguss.

Opposite: This temperance imagery portrays the ever more popular absinthe as "The Green Peril."

Le Péril vert : L'Absinthe.
Collection T. Bianco.

Unlikely Bedfellows

Absinthe makes you crazy and criminal, provokes epilepsy and tuberculosis, and has killed thousands of French people. It makes a ferocious beast of man, a martyr of woman, and a degenerate of the infant. It disorganizes and ruins the family and menaces the future of the country.

– Temperance petition, 1907

While the late nineteenth century gave rise to bohemian counterculture and unconventional thinking, it also gave rise to its antithesis – the temperance movement. Temperance represented a well-organized answer to the excesses of drinking that were a hallmark of the times. The members of this movement consisted largely of evangelical organizations, as well as women who endured abuse, divorce, widowhood, or who had witnessed the demise of a family member as a result of alcoholism or substance abuse.

Temperance thinking was not simply a phenomenon of European culture; it was simultaneously manifested across the Atlantic, particularly in the United States. These groups slowly but steadily gained support from a sympathetic public and government alike. And as with any agenda to curtail freedom, the temperance movement needed a scapegoat upon which to focus its anger and justify its intent. There was none that proved to be riper for the picking than the potent green liquid that had become the national rage. Not only was absinthe renowned as the liquor that lubricated the inhibitions of the masses, but the seductive drink was well known to be that which fueled the glorified indulgences of the group most reviled by the temperance movement: those decadent bohemians. The scandalous nature of artists, poets, slackers, and prostitutes had undermined the old establishment, and threatened the very core of the French nation. Clearly,

the temperance league was unappreciative of what Hemingway would describe as "that opaque, bitter, tongue-numbing, brain-warming, stomach-warming, idea-changing liquid alchemy."

The temperance movement wasn't alone in its desire to demonize absinthe. The formidable economic and political leviathan that was the wine industry was recovering, finding itself opposed to the popularity of the green spirit, a glass of which could be had in a café for what was described as one-third the cost of a loaf of bread. An old Sanskrit proverb promotes the idea that "the enemy of my enemy is my friend." This was the situation in France that brought wine and teetotaling zealots together in a smear campaign waged against absinthe. Over the course of several decades, these two groups collaborated to fund widely distributed propaganda that portrayed absinthe as a poison and squarely to blame for society's ills. They labeled any person displaying the effects of alcoholism an absinthe drinker, and solicited the aid of sympathizing politicians in an effort to ban the scourge. By the dawn of the twentieth century, years of rhetoric were beginning to have an effect. The contentious issue had become a powder keg. The only missing element was the spark that would ignite it, and that was poised to come.

Opposite: A rare drawing in which a pair of gentlemen admire two women who appear fixated upon preparing a glass of absinthe.

Right: A combination of heavy spoon holders, also known as troncs de comptoir in French. These typically sat upon the bar, awaiting patrons to pluck spoons in anticipation of louching glasses of absinthe.

Last Call

Following the brutal "absinthe murder" in 1905, Switzerland was the first country to experience an absinthe ban. This regional ban could not be contained. On the contrary, it sparked a succession of similar actions, culminating in a ban that was written into the Swiss constitution in 1908, which in turn effectively banned the production and sale of absinthe in the entire country as of October 7, 1910.

The Absinthe Murder

The typically pastoral Swiss countryside would provide the backdrop for a brutal murder that reverberated across Switzerland and beyond. On an August day in 1905, farm laborer Jean Lanfray awoke as usual, bolstering himself at breakfast with copious amounts of wine and brandy. For lunch, Lanfray returned and continued his drinking binge, which again included wine, brandy, a couple of crème de menthes, and finally, two glasses of absinthe. It was during this session that Lanfray found himself in a heated argument with his pregnant wife regarding the waxing of his boots. In a fit of drunken rage, Lanfray grabbed a rifle, executed his wife, then subsequently his two daughters. He then levied the weapon against himself, and fired a round into his jaw, which turned out nonfatal.

News of this heinous incident spread like wildfire. Labeled the "absinthe murder," news accounts sensationalized the event by placing the blame squarely upon the two ounces of absinthe Lanfray consumed at the end of his binge. Despite the absurdity of the notion in consideration of the volume of alcohol Lanfray had consumed that day, public sentiment quickly interpreted the incident as a clear-cut case of "absinthe madness."

The publicity was quickly exploited by a temperance action that secured some 82,000 signatures in support of banning absinthe, which led lawmakers in the French-speaking canton of Vaud to vote in favor of banning absinthe in May 1906. This was the first domino to fall.

What was particularly significant about the nationwide Swiss prohibition isn't that it was the first. In fact, Belgium and Brazil had enacted bans on the curious green liquor in 1906, and the Netherlands followed suit in 1909. What made the Swiss ban particularly problematic was the fact that a significant portion of absinthe in the global market originated from that country. It was internationally noted that

Sous ces traits élégants, d'allure distinguée,
Reconnais-toi, mon cher, quand tu es en bordée.

the Swiss passed a constitutional law that eliminated a segment of their own industry. Also worthy of note was the realization that the Swiss ban had the effect of leaving France as the only remaining major producer of the spirit.

The banning of absinthe in Switzerland set a precedent that encouraged other governments to follow suit. Absinthe was now widely viewed as a chronic threat to public health. Sensing that the tide was turning in its favor, the temperance movement stepped up the pressure by distributing everything from huge posters to postcards that depicted skeletons and other macabre figures as dealers of absinthe, ruin, and death. Gradually, this ongoing campaign took a toll on public sentiment – in spite of the fact that in the years that followed the Swiss ban, consumption in France and elsewhere continued to steadily increase – as did political pressure exerted by the wine industry to do away with its prime competitor.

Meanwhile, controversy brewed within the US government concerning the growing popularity of what was oft referred to as the "green curse of France." Just a few years before, in 1906, the federal government had taken an active stance in guarding public health with the Pure Food and Drugs Act, which prohibited the production and sale of food and drugs that were deemed misbranded,

Opposite: This amusing postcard is a reminder: "Under these elegant features, distinguished in appearance, admit, my dear fellow, when you are on the fringe."

Right: A postcard ad for Pel-Temps absinthe, featuring a gentleman relaxing with his trusty pipe and a glass of absinthe.

Après la bataille du 5 juillet 1908   Nach der Schlacht vom 5. Juli 1908

adulterated, or deleterious. In the same spirit of that law, the US Department of Agriculture passed Food Inspection Decision 147 in June 1912, which effectively eliminated the production, importation, and sale of absinthe, by declaring the spirit in violation of the Pure Food and Drugs Act in light of its "deleterious properties" and the fact that it had been banned in various other countries.

Finally, having witnessed the ban of the controversial French spirit in many countries, the subject finally came to a head within the French government. Giving in to the pressures of temperance and the wine industry, the government passed a ban on the sale and consumption of absinthe in August 1914, with a ban on the production going into effect in January 1915. Perhaps it seemed like a relatively minor event, as the clouds of war had begun to rain upon the French nation in July 1914. The new law and intensifying war saw the large Pernod Fils distillery converted into a military hospital. And while the French ban on absinthe is invariably mentioned as a historical event, far less frequently is it mentioned that France shortly thereafter passed a ban on all high-proof spirits, to prevent the trenches from being filled with drunken soldiers. But, to preserve morale, every fighting man was guaranteed his ration of wine. Such was how the Belle Époque came to an abrupt terminus.

Opposite: An advertisement for Absinthe Terminus, in which the lady confesses, "It's my little sin."

Above: This image depicts the "battle of July 5, 1908," whereupon the Swiss people voted to ban absinthe, which went into effect in 1910.

3

The
Dark Ages

Post Mortem

In less than a decade, absinthe went from being one of the world's signature spirits to a state of virtual nonexistence. With the bans passed by what were overwhelmingly the two largest producing countries, Switzerland and France, the fabled green liquor was effectively extirpated from the global market. And while there were a handful of small producers in other nations, these were more often than not ersatz versions of the traditional drink, of poor quality, and globally insignificant. Nevertheless, other countries continued passing bans on the vilified liquid, with Chile enacting a ban in 1916, and Germany and Italy passing bans in 1923 and 1926, respectively.

When World War I finally ended, France had suffered casualties of more than 1.5 million, or more than 4 percent of its population. Gone was the prewar gaiety that earned Paris the reputation of being the cultural center of the universe. Upon the gradual restoration of the production of high-proof spirits, the rules for anise-flavored liquors were stern. A strict limitation of 40 percent ABV was mandated, the spirit had to contain at least 450 grams of sugar per liter(!), and it could not be green. And while the old Pernod Fils company and its distillery were now relegated to the history books, its name was amalgamated into a conglomerate and revived for a sugary anise liqueur produced under these conditions.

Opposite: This image is typical of temperance artwork that aimed to demonize the green spirit.

Maison PERNOD Fils
3. - Wagon réservoir pour transport d'alcool

Curiously enough, the original Pernod Fils name and labeling would soon reappear on a bottle of absinthe, distilled not in Pontarlier, but in Tarragona, Spain, under the banner of Pernod S.A. The Spanish entity was originally founded in 1912, and began producing the immensely popular, but then-defunct Swiss brand Edouard Pernod, which it did for more than twenty years. At some point after the First World War, the Tarragona distillery began producing absinthe under the original Pernod Fils label. In their earlier bottlings, the Spanish versions of these original Swiss and French absinthes were relatively good facsimiles of the venerable brands. They were

Top left: Pernod Fils printed a series of postcards depicting various aspects of the distillery. This one boasts the company's branded railcars used to transport the wine spirit employed as the base of the drink.

Above: Many of these wooden-framed advertising lithographs were produced by Pernod Fils, and were made to be hung on café walls.

Opposite: Although pastis is often associated with absinthe, the two spirits are very different. Pastis is a sugary liqueur that contains no wormwood, is almost invariably cold-mixed from commercial flavorings, and is artificially colored.

gradually industrialized with the passage of time, with far less esteemed bottlings persisting until around 1970. Concurrent with this effort were at least several other Spanish absinthes from various distilleries that arose to fill the void created by the French and Swiss bans. Like their Pernod Tarragona–branded brethren, the early bottlings by independent Spanish distilleries were of artisanal quality, gradually giving way to the post–World War II trend of cheapening and industrialization that still persists today.

Gone but Not Forgotten

By 1930, the world had witnessed a rash of bans on absinthe, the ravages of a world war, and the onset of a global economic crisis. In France, the national drink was gone, and a void in the marketplace was created in its wake. Aiming to take advantage of the situation, numerous substitutes appeared, all attempting to become the next big thing. These included various aperitif wines, bitter liqueurs, and most notably, a signature anise-flavored spirit commercialized by Paul Ricard that became pastis. It was intended to be a pastiche (imitation) for a sugared absinthe drink. Originally an artisanally distilled anise liqueur infused with licorice root, it too has been industrialized into the cold-compounded, artificially colored versions that exist today.

Meanwhile, the Americans endured a disastrous thirteen-year experiment that was known as Prohibition. Having finally come to terms with the reality

that total temperance was a social failure, Prohibition was repealed in 1933. And upon blowing the dust off of their old cocktail books, it became obvious that cocktails that called for absinthe (and there were many) could no longer be made, because there was nothing available that closely mimicked the flavor of the virtually extinct spirit. Perhaps nowhere was this more apparent than in what had been the absinthe capital of North America – New Orleans, where signature cocktails such as Sazeracs and absinthe frappés were now devoid of a key ingredient.

Swiss Bootleggers

Back in the rolling hills of the Val-de-Travers region of Switzerland, amidst the backdrop of sleepy agricultural villages where Dr. Ordinaire had first popularized his tasty medicine, the Swiss constitutional ban wasn't being followed by everyone. In the years that followed, the local taste for absinthe was not forgotten. Clandestine distillers resumed small-scale production of the perfumed spirit in the basements of homes and in the shady depths of the forest. It was within this environment that the final infusion of herbs, responsible

The Holy Herb

J.M. Legendre was a native New Orleanian who had spent time in France during World War I. Upon the repeal of Prohibition, he received the first license to produce high-proof spirits in the southern United States. Wasting no time, he released in 1934 a rectified herbal liqueur labeled "Legendre Absinthe," albeit devoid of the requisite *Artemisia absinthium*. Like absinthe, the spirit was bottled at elevated (120) proof, and exhibited a flavor profile that approached that of the original spirit. It wasn't long, however, before Legendre drew the ire of the government, who struck down his product on grounds of mislabeling. Forced to rename his spirit, Legendre chose the name "Herbsaint," ostensibly in reference to *Herbe Sainte*, the creole French term for the "holy herb," *Artemisia absinthium*. Legendre wasn't without competition, however, as L.E. Jung and Wulff, which actually distilled absinthe in New Orleans prior to the ban, released its own substitute that was bottled and sold under the brand Milky Way.

The regional popularity of Legendre's Herbsaint effectively filled the void left by the eradication of absinthe. As one advertising slogan wisely advised: "Herbsaint – always used when absinthe is called for." Unfortunately for Legendre, his absinthe substitute was not widely distributed outside of its native region, where it remained a cultural icon. Eventually, it too would be modernized and industrialized into a shadow of its former self. In 2009, however, on the seventy-fifth anniversary of J.M. Legendre's original incarnation, the Sazerac Company re-released a bottling of Legendre's original recipe, which remains in production, and is true to the original flavor profile.

for contributing to absinthe its distinguishable green tint, became regularly omitted in favor of tossing all the herbs in the distilling pot, the result being a crystal-clear spirit – widely speculated to be for reasons of evading detection. Whereas any green anise-flavored liquor was almost certainly identifiable as absinthe, something clear remains ambiguous. The bootleggers developed this style quietly, and under the radar of federal officials.

The lighter, clear absinthe that was almost always individually distilled and bottled at lower proof became referred to by a clandestine nickname – La Bleue. And while rarely spoken about with anything greater than a whisper, this illegally produced mountain hooch became the pride of the local valley community, which even today seems fairly well insulated from the treachery of the outside world. Over the course of the decades that followed, the flavor

Right: Another of a series of four black cat postcards by Absinthe Bourgeois.

profile of the bootlegged Swiss product quietly evolved into a style distinctly different from that of its Belle Époque predecessor, and thus La Bleue remained a quiet, agricultural commodity of the Val-de-Travers for the ninety-five-year duration of the Swiss ban. So entrenched was it as a hush-hush icon of the region that some locals were disappointed upon the eventual repeal of the Swiss ban.

Green Fairy Tales

After a second world war and the decades that followed, the epic odyssey of absinthe gradually regressed into something akin to mythical fable, buried deep within the pages of an old novel. The virtual absence and inaccessibility of the spirit fostered an environment that eventually gave rise to spurious theories and gross misinformation. Here and there, an occasional magazine article would appear that sensationalized the drink as an evil liquid that brought hallucinations and madness to all who tasted it.

The popularity of illicit drugs among the new bohemian culture of the 1960s and 1970s brought with it a gentle resurgence in interest in the extinct green spirit as a potential source of mind-bending effects. By the end of the 1970s, informative articles on the subject of absinthe were mostly befitting the trash heap of pulp fiction, accomplishing little except adding insult to injury. But of all the speculation and theories regarding the allegations made against absinthe, there was none so widely accepted as the thujone theory.

Opposite: Couvet, Switzerland is located in the heart of the Val-de-Travers, and is considered the birthplace of absinthe.

Right: Alexandre Graverol's watercolor (ca. 1900) again shows a floating head of Paul Verlaine at top with a green goddess, glass of absinthe, and assorted occult imagery.

Thujone's Theory

Thujone is an aromatic monoterpene, which is a class of compounds found in the essences of various plants. The pure compound is a clear liquid at room temperature with a heady menthol-like odor. Thujone is produced by many different plants, including various wormwoods and tarragon from the *Artemisia* genus, sages from the *Salvia* genus, cedars from the *Thuja* genus, and various other botanicals and herbs. And notably, thujone often occurs in significant concentrations within absinthe's namesake herb, *Artemisia absinthium*. Predictably, foods and beverages containing these plants (or their extracts) often contain traces of this compound.

Long ago, those who sought to smear the popular green liquor had to find something wrong with it. By conveniently singling out *Artemisia absinthium* as

a key ingredient invariably found in absinthe and not much of anything else, detractors of absinthe were quick to accuse this botanical of being poisonous, invoking the results of Dr. Magnan's animal experiments, in which guinea pigs and others were exposed to high concentrations of oil of wormwood in order to demonstrate the theory. The logic was that if something in grand wormwood could be demonstrated as poisonous, then surely the liquor that is derived from it must be equally poisonous, and therefore the source of all of humankind's ruin.

The human brain produces a substance known as GABA (gamma-aminobutyric acid). GABA's primary function is to inhibit nerve impulses, likened to brakes on a car in traffic. Without GABA, our nerve impulses fire too easily – signals become less controlled. In-vitro laboratory studies have shown that thujone can block the brain-cell receptors that normally pick up GABA. Thus, the "brakes" release, permitting nerve impulses to fire uncontrollably. This observation led many to assume that thujone is "psychoactive," and therefore absinthe is also "psychoactive." Furthermore, it was hypothesized in the 1970s that thujone bound to the brain's cannabinoid receptors, resulting in sensations similar to those experienced by smoking marijuana. This theory was based on the similarities in molecular structure between thujone and tetrahydrocannabinol (the active component in marijuana). These hypotheses were often invoked without reservation to reach the "logical" conclusion that absinthe was a dangerous, addictive substance that delivered illicit drug-like psychoactive effects.

Opposite left: Artemisia absinthium *contains thujone, which can cause convulsions and kidney failure when ingested in large amounts.*

Opposite: A hand-colored print depicts an elegant monkey smoking a pipe and sipping an absinthe.

Above: Byrrh quinquina was one of several bitter wine aperitifs that angled for a slice of absinthe's market share by promoting itself as a healthy alternative. Here, a soldier kicks a skeletonized waiter carrying a glass of absinthe.

So popular were these beliefs that by the 1990s, they were widely quoted as gospel truth in articles in periodicals and books about the once popular green elixir. These notions were sometimes sensationalized to extrapolate a view of nineteenth-century French café culture as chaotic scenes wherein throngs of people were milling about, experiencing LSD-like hallucinations and general ecstasy. If there was a low point, it may be an incident reported by the *New England Journal of Medicine* in 1997 in which a young man, believing oil of wormwood was analogous to absinthe, imbibed about ten milliliters of the substance in hopes that thujone, a convulsant, would provide exhilarating effects. The result was uncontrollable tonic and clonic seizures and incoherence, followed by a variety of medical issues, including renal failure. Clearly, there was no discernible connection between this horrific, life-threatening episode and the once-fashionable spirit that fueled generations of art and culture, at one time lauded as the national drink of France.

Science to the Rescue

Perhaps the first brick to be chipped from the construct of stubborn absinthe myths came in the form of a scientific study in 1997 by Meschler, Marsh, and Howlett (International Cannabinoid Research Society) that conclusively proved thujone does not bind with cannabinoid receptors, as often quoted by popular lore. This effectively dissociated absinthe from anything related to cannabis or THC.

A few years later, a resurgence in interest in the fabled green spirit began to bring forth full, sealed antique bottles of pre-ban absinthes from the collections of various old European wine cellars. The occasional discovery of dusty, unmolested bottles representing the finest absinthe brands of the Belle Époque made possible scientific analysis of the venerable spirit, which had never before been performed. Beginning in 2000, independent investigators such as Breaux (the editor) in the United States, Hutton in the UK, and Lachenmeier in Germany were respectively reporting similar results – these old bottles, as well as recent distillations carried out in strict accordance with antique distillation treatises, were yielding nothing damning with respect to the content of thujone or anything else deemed convulsant, psychoactive, or otherwise deleterious.

Left: A miniature Deniset absinthe bottle

Opposite: The so-called "Absinthe Professors" by Paul Renouard, 1889

In 2004, in another study using human subjects, Dettling and Grass (*Journal of Studies on Alcohol*) demonstrated those subjects unable to distinguish between test samples that contained exponential differences in thujone concentration. But the final nail in the coffin for the thujone theory would come in 2008, with the publishing of a peer-reviewed study by Lachenmeier, Nathan-Maister, Breaux, et al. (*Journal of Agricultural and Food Chemistry*) that examined a number of notable pre-ban absinthes, revealing that none of them exhibited a concentration of thujone or anything else that would present a threat to health. These studies over the course of a decade catalyzed a paradigm shift in the understanding of absinthe that would contribute to its heralded return.

Top: Two absinthe spoons crudely fashioned in the field ca. 1914, during World War I. The spoons were fabricated by whatever metals were available at the time.

Above: Branded absinthe spoons were common at the time, and featured a variety of popular absinthes of the day.

Opposite: A vintage newspaper illustration dramatically depicts the "dangers of absinthe."

Root of the Problem

Absinths of bad quality are often made, some of them manufactured without distillation and with essences to replace the plants and seeds which are used in the genuine process.

– Beverages and Their Adulteration,
Harvey W. Wiley (1919)

It was no secret as far back as the mid-nineteenth century that cheap, adulterated versions of the spirit were in commerce, particularly in France, where absinthe was incredibly popular. This problem was described in books on distillation, distillers of quality absinthes, and even noted by journalists who observed unexpected irregularities, such as a metallic taste left in one's mouth. These absinthes were concocted in urban warehouses, often from industrial alcohol, commercial oils and essences, and even metallic salts – none of which belong in any traditionally distilled absinthe. The production of such imposters was possible because unlike cognac, champagne, cheeses, and every regional French wine, there was no appellation to protect absinthe, no laws, not even a basic legal definition. This allowed virtually anything to be put into a bottle and sold as absinthe, and many profiteers did exactly that. These were the days before basic food and beverage standards existed, which is why brand consciousness for discriminating absinthe consumers was the rule of the day. *Caveat emptor.*

As absinthes exported to the French colonies, the Americas, and elsewhere were almost always the larger, respectable brands, this relegated the phenomenon of absinthism, the kind of alcoholism that people believed was related specifically to drinking absinthe, as mostly a continental French problem. Additionally, as mentioned in Chapter 2, a recent scientific study noted that much of what was originally diagnosed as absinthism appears to be complications associated with ordinary alcoholism. Another important observation is that a century after the ban, dusty pre-ban bottles of absinthe that occasionally emerge from the cellars of old European estates are invariably respectable, traditionally distilled examples of the spirit. Those who possessed homes with cellars were generally those of reasonable financial means, and those persons had little incentive to buy and store inexpensive, adulterated versions of the drink. If there is any social group that paid the price for the cheap, inferior brands of absinthe that permeated the lower rungs of the market, it was those of modest means, particularly poor alcoholics who imbibed copious volumes of these unfit spirits with bizarre, albeit predictable consequences. Meanwhile, it cannot be ignored that millions around the world imbibed the potent green elixir on a frequent, if not regular basis, and lived productive lives without experiencing anything unusual.

4

THE LONG ROAD HOME: ABSINTHE RETURNS

An interesting event happened in 1988, when the founding-member European Union (EU) nations standardized their food and beverage laws. This had the effect of sweeping aside the individual regulations in favor of a new set of modern standards. In doing so, it quietly lifted the old bans on absinthe passed by individual nations the better part of a century before. And interestingly enough, no one noticed... well, almost no one.

Shortly thereafter in 1989, the Velvet Revolution brought about the fall of the hard-line Communist regime in Czechoslovakia. In the years that followed, European tourists discovered Prague as one of the most beautiful cities on the continent, and also one that was a relative bargain compared to similar cities in western Europe. This brought considerable holiday traffic to the Czech capital – a center of culture, music, and art that was largely closed to Westerners for several decades. The Czechs are renowned for their beer, as well as for native spirits and liqueurs such as slivovitz and Becherovka. Curious Westerners soon noticed that in Czech spirit shops, among the bottles of inexpensive, ersatz liquors hailing from the communist times, were bottles of a blue-green liquid labeled "Absinth." Many tourists bought these bottles of "absinth" while on vacation and returned home with them, believing them to be synonymous with the fabled Franco-Swiss spirit of yore. Eventually, this would prove to be a source of considerable confusion.

Opposite: The historic Combier distillery in Saumur, France, was constructed by Gustave Eiffel. The original nineteenth-century stills used to distill absinthe beginning in the 1880s are still in service today.

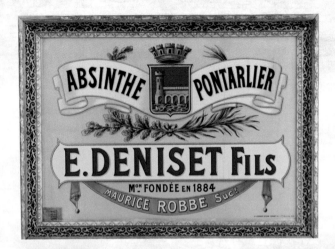

Above: An old Deniset absinthe label, atop a hanging placard that advertises Absinthe Premier Fils.

Right: Les Fils d'Emile Pernot is one of two surviving original absinthe distilleries in Pontarlier, France, the other being Distillerie Armand Guy.

Opposite: A postcard glimpse into the Absinthe Bourgeois distillery.

Meanwhile in France, the 1990s came and went without much fanfare. It wasn't until the end of the decade that swelling interest in the spirit urged a couple of French distillers from the old absinthe capital of Pontarlier to delve into current law, only to find nothing in the new code that would preclude

them from distilling *Artemisia absinthium*. Sure, there had been until that point a handful of cheap, industrial Spanish offerings and a few artificially colored, sugary French liqueurs that attempted to present themselves as something akin to genuine absinthe, but aside from the very obscure Segarra (45% ABV) brand of Spanish *"absenta"* from the distillery of Julian Segarra, the marketplace was completely devoid of any artisanally crafted spirit that could rightfully be deemed absinthe.

It wouldn't be until the dawn of the new century, in 2001, when François Guy of the venerable Armand Guy distillery in Pontarlier launched its François Guy (45% ABV) brand of absinthe, which became the first legally produced, artisanally crafted absinthe sold in France in almost a century. Not long thereafter, another Pontarlier distillery, Les Fils d'Emile Pernot, would launch their Vieux Pontarlier (65% ABV) brand. Other French brands would follow, but most were simply cold-mixed from flavorings and green dye.

For a period of several years, aside from the seldom-seen Segarra brand from Spain, the French François Guy and Vieux Pontarlier would be the only commercial absinthes on the planet that were completely natural and distilled directly from botanicals in the traditional method. And while one might suppose that the country to which absinthe was once granted the title of the "national drink" would warmly embrace its return, mere mention of the word *absinthe* was viewed with sharp skepticism and a jaundiced eye just about everywhere outside of Pontarlier.

When absinthe was quietly relegalized in the EU back in 1988, the event didn't go entirely unnoticed. Someone in the French Ministry of Health, upon realizing the effect of the new EU laws, noiselessly passed a decree that deemed that any absinthe-like spirit that contained more than a paltry amount of thujone, fenchone (from fennel), or pinocamphone (from hyssop) would be legally determined to be absinthe, and its producers subject to all of the draconian penalties of the original ban. To avoid legal complications, French producers had to adhere to the content restrictions, while labeling their spirits *boisson spiritueuse aux plantes d'absinthe* (alcoholic drink with absinthe plants) as a workaround to avoid calling the spirit "absinthe," which was illegal. In 2007, Messrs. T.A. Breaux (author) and Franck Choisne of the Combier distillery found themselves on the wrong side of this rule when Breaux's Jade Liqueurs brand of absinthes were deemed to contain enough fennel to legally qualify as genuine absinthes under the French definition. This resulted in thousands of liters of aging distillate being seized by French customs, thousands of euros in fines, and the dubious honor of being the last producers in France charged and fined under the terms of the 1915 French absinthe ban. Being dissatisfied with the outcome, the Combier group assembled a legal team to challenge the basis for the decree. After giving the matter reconsideration, the French Ministry of Health relented and struck down the rule. As a result, the last vestiges of the original French ban were finally swept aside in 2009, which allowed French distillers to use the standalone term *absinthe* on the label, as well as include sufficient botanicals such as fennel without worrying they would find themselves in violation of a technicality. Clearly, times and views were gradually changing, even in the nation where absinthe had been most vilified.

Just across the border in Switzerland, the end of the twentieth century likewise witnessed a resurgence in interest in the spirit that had been a source of pride for the folks of the Val-de-Travers. In fact, a festival to commemorate the old spirit was held in the sleepy village of Boveresse, which became an annual gathering. And while the tiny pot stills squirreled away in basements kept churning out clear, perfumed distillates of absinthe one liter at a time for the purpose of lubricating festival-goers who arrived from faraway places, none could be had except through a daisy chain of whispers. Surely, many local folks recalled a scandalous, highly publicized event in 1983 when a Swiss chef from a restaurant in nearby Neuchâtel served visiting French president François Mitterand a dessert he called *Soufflé glacé à la fée verte*, suspected to contain absinthe, only to receive a subsequent visit from the national police and a fine for causing a commotion. It is as if one dipped his foot to test the waters, only to have it bitten off by a piranha.

Opposite: The Combier distillery in the Loire Valley is one of the very few original pre-ban absinthe distilleries that has remained in continuous operation to the present day.

Right: An undated black-and-white image taken many years ago shows the interior of the distillery.

Below: The interior of the Combier distillery as it appears today, largely unchanged with Eiffel's ironwork still present. Note the addition of two 1,100 liter nineteenth-century absinthe stills (far right), obtained from Pernod Fils following the liquidation of its Pontarlier distillery.

Above: A drawing by famous French painter, printmaker, and sculptor Jean-François Raffaëlli (1850–1924) of a mildly tattered man, sitting at a rustic table with a glass of absinthe

Above right: A trio of antique water carafes – the center item is designed to allow for careful dripping, while the piece at the left has a circumferential metal band where it unscrews into upper and lower halves to add a chunk of ice to the water.

Fortunately, the advent of modern science had proven worthy of protecting public health from beverages deemed harmful, which gradually brought about a more *laissez-faire* attitude, particularly by the local authorities. Emboldened by a more sensible view of the spirit, as well as the fact that their brethren just across the French side of the border were having all the fun, the inhabitants of the Canton of Vaud petitioned the Swiss federal government to amend the constitution, which finally became official in 2005. This enabled once-clandestine distillers to emerge from the shadows, apply for amnesty, and obtain distillation licenses to legitimize their once

bootlegged hooch. The change in the Swiss law allowed early commercialized brands such as Kübler (45% ABV), the aptly named La Clandestine (53% ABV), and DuVallon (53% ABV) to make themselves known in the marketplace.

But while absinthe was experiencing a revival throughout Europe, all was not well in this new paradise. Having realized that tourists were willing to pay good money for bottles of artificially colored blue-green liquid so long as it had the word *absinthe* on the label, profiteers were quick to exploit public ignorance in the hopes of making a profit. As such, these imposters began surfacing across central and eastern Europe, from "distilleries" that possessed no stills. Most amounted to nothing more than bad-tasting flavored vodka colored with artificial dyes. Others consisted of high-proof alcohol with a few pinches of herb dust added to the bottle. Most were marketed using seductive imagery, while falsely promising to be produced from antique French or Swiss recipes, and pledged hallucinations.

A Flaming Disappointment

One important hallmark of inferior absinthes is that few would louche (cloud) upon the addition of ice water, which rendered the original French service useless. To distract the consumer from significant disappointment, a new ritual was invented whereby absinthe was poured over a sugar cube, which was ignited and allowed to burn before being stirred into the glass. Such distractions were invented to lull the consumer away from recognizing a rip-off.

To make matters worse, Hollywood adopted the false theatrics, with films such as *Moulin Rouge* and *From Hell* depicting absurd scenes, replete with flaming absinthe. Meanwhile, not one historic painting, drawing, photograph, or writing makes note of anyone setting absinthe alight, and with good reason – it ruins the drink, and it never happened. Such misinformation and antics had a particularly devastating effect in the UK, where the category was being killed as fast as it was being created, making absinthe reduced to rubbish, a flaming shot suitable only for drunken hooligans.

All this was made possible by one omission that was as problematic in the nineteenth century as it proved to be in the early twenty-first century – that,

unlike Scotch whiskey or London gin, there was no legal definition for absinthe. This allowed anything to be put into a bottle and labeled *absinthe*, and undoubtedly just about anything was. Only one nation passed a legal standard for absinthe, Switzerland, upon repealing the ban in 2005. As a result, none of the usual offenders could legally be sold there.

Meanwhile, the repeal of the Swiss ban in 2005 left the United States as the last bastion of the old effort to eradicate absinthe. And while the creation of the FDA (Food and Drug Administration) and modernization of food and beverage laws in 1968 technically cleared the way for absinthe's return, the TTB (Alcohol and Tobacco Tax and Trade Bureau) wanted no part of it, primarily due to the waves of bad press surrounding the cheap imposters that plagued the European market, and the irresponsible false advertising with which they were associated. This would remain the status quo for several years, with numerous brands of absinthe attempting to obtain approval in the States, only to be rejected, thus leaving the US market with only a few artificially colored, sugary liqueurs as second-rate substitutes, *Artemisia absinthium* being entirely absent. Under the direction of Messrs. Jared Gurfein and T.A. Breaux, and following months of discussion, the TTB agreed to grant permission on March 5, 2007 to the French Lucid (62% ABV) brand from Viridian Spirits (Combier), the first genuine absinthe to be approved for distribution and sale in the United States since 1912. This was followed over the next few months by the Swiss Kübler (53% ABV) brand, and the first US brand produced since the ban, St. George (60% ABV).

The US market proved to be particularly receptive to the rebirth of the notorious Franco-Swiss spirit, as the relaunch was greeted with considerable press and fanfare. And thanks to the enormous repository of information that was the internet, Americans were largely spared the wrath of the fakes and phonies that plagued Europe. With a few

notable exceptions, the US market was commanded by artisanally crafted absinthes, which effectively preserved the reputation of the spirit. Furthermore, US labeling guidelines require the disclosure of artificial colorants (e.g., FD&C Yellow No. 5) in the label's fine print, which enables consumers to have an easier time of weeding out the cheaply made, industrialized brands that are angling to profit from the revitalized interest in the category. The lifting of the US ban and educational efforts to keep the imposters at bay did much to ensure absinthe's place in the craft cocktail revival that was just beginning to gain steam as the first decade of the twenty-first century was drawing to a close.

Opposite: A freshly distilled glass of Jade 1901 Absinthe Supérieure

Below: Vintage absinthe's influence over the current scene is palpable. While some contemporary absinthes put a completely different spin on their flavors, others strive to capture the essence of absinthe from days gone by. The postcard on the right is a modern illustration of the classic "It's my health!" Cusenier Oxygénée absinthe postcard dating back to the nineteenth century.

5

ACCOUTREMENTS and ANTIQUES

The popularity of absinthe in the ubiquitous cafés and bistros of France inevitably spawned a wealth of items dedicated to serving the spirit in the most traditional manner. Some were fairly simple and utilitarian, some elegant and ornate, and some downright gimmicky. One aspect they all shared in common was that they were designed for the explicit purpose of serving absinthe and little of anything else. The absinthe glasses, spoons, and fountains that once permeated the French nation were hallmarks of a sophisticated and fashionable society. Following the crippling bans of the twentieth century, however, these now-obsolete items were shelved, packed away, repurposed, or forgotten altogether. By the latter decades of the century, they had been relegated to the category of "old bistro ware," only to be found piecemeal, gathering dust on the shelves of continental flea markets. By that time, the spirit had been gone for so long that few knew much about absinthe, or cared.

A gradual change would begin with the publication of a French language book by Marie-Claude Delahaye in 1983 entitled *L'absinthe: Histoire de la fée Verte*. Now curator of the Musée de l'Absinthe (44 rue Callé, Auvers-sur-Oise, France), Delahaye's book provided the first modern reference guide to vintage bistro items uniquely associated with serving the green spirit. Delahaye's organization and imagery provided a basis of identification that allowed these old pieces to be differentiated

Opposite: French painter Jean Béraud was famous for his paintings of Paris nightlife. This painting, Les Joueurs de Backgammon (The Backgammon Players) *from 1909 showcases his humor in his gentle mockery of life during the Belle Époque. Although the beautiful woman does not appear to be drinking absinthe, she has the familiar blank gaze associated with absinthe imbibers.*

from their peers. The benefit of positive identification allowed *brocanteurs* to present these items not merely as old barware, but as absinthe accoutrements, which had the effect of bolstering their value. Eventually, a trickle of these items would make their way into the hands of antiques dealers outside of Europe, where they aroused curiosity about the spirit and the sordid epic that surrounded it. And because absinthe accoutrements had now become identifiable, this made collecting such things a practical hobby.

As absinthe serving items were beginning to trickle out of dusty storage bins and into the hands

of a sprinkling of collectors who emerged toward the end of the twentieth century, Barnaby Conrad III published a book that would be a game changer for Anglophones. *Absinthe: History in a Bottle*, was first published in 1988 (Chronicle Books), filling a substantial void with information about absinthe that had been sorely lacking in the English-speaking world. Conrad's detailed, finely illustrated work would serve as a lone bright spot that shone light upon a dark, widely misunderstood mystery.

What Delahaye's work had done for absinthe accoutrements, Conrad's work did for the story of the infamous green spirit, and it is undoubtedly

Right: These antique water pitchers were used in preparing a traditional French/Swiss absinthe. The center pitcher features the phrase: "Messieurs, C'est l'Heure" ("Gentlemen, it's time"), referring to the October 7, 1910, ban on absinthe in Switzerland. The clock points to a few minutes before midnight.

Opposite left: An Absinthe Bourgeois metal inkwell

Opposite right: A gift box for customers of Terminus, one of the more popular absinthe brands during the turn of the last century. It reads: "L'Absinthe Terminus à sés fidèles Consommateurs" ("Absinthe Terminus to their loyal Customers"). The box probably held tobacco.

responsible for launching the modern-day curiosity about and interest in the misunderstood green liquor.

In addition to the books by Delahaye and Conrad, the gradual appearance of commercial absinthes available via web retailers in the late 1990s, despite ranging from weak to deplorable in quality, caused a resurgence of interest in absinthe-related vintage items. For those living outside of continental Europe, however, obtaining these pieces required some effort. The end of the twentieth century, which saw the beginning of annual Swiss and French absinthe festivals in the Val-de-Travers and Pontarlier, provided bountiful flea markets of antique wares for collectors

such as Betina Wittels (author) who were willing to make the trip. In the United States, a trickling of absinthe antiques began appearing on ebay, while visitors to New Orleans found a steady stream of absinthe glasses and spoons appearing in the display windows of French culinary antiques specialist Lucullus, at 610 Chartres Street.

The tools of the absintheur were essentially a spoon, a glass, a sugar cube, chilled water, and of course, absinthe. These accoutrements apply when serving absinthe in the traditional Franco-Swiss fashion, which is simply the metering of cold water to the neat spirit until the taste is deemed appropriate.

And while this is simple in principle, the fashionable preparation is akin to the Japanese tea ceremony. The elegance and attention to detail afforded by *objets d'art* associated with absinthe imply something of greater importance than the bistro- and barware typical of the period.

Glassware
(*Les Verres*)

When a patron ordered an absinthe in a French or Swiss establishment, that person was simply given a glass with a dose of liquor, to be finished by the patron the way they liked. Glassware dedicated to serving this purpose was crafted in France for the better part of a century, from the time absinthe was rapidly rising in popularity in the mid-1800s until the ban.

Absinthe glasses were typically made of flint glass, blown into a mold by hand, and relatively heavy in construction for reasons of durability. Absinthe glasses were of various styles, ranging from parfait-style glasses to stems, but all reflective of the period.

The designs of some types of absinthe glassware are such that they may have been used for additional purposes, such as the Swirl, Egg, Chope Yvonne, Mazagran, Lyonnaise, and East styles. The larger examples of these styles are those intended to accommodate a shot of absinthe plus the addition of at least several volumes of water often needed to complete the drink. To facilitate the job of the bartender even

further, some absinthe glasses possess a utilitarian design element in the form of a distinct feature or etched line that indicates where to pour the shot.

Meanwhile, certain other styles of glassware, most notably the Cordon, Reservoir, and Pontarlier styles, were used exclusively for absinthe. These styles are more distinctive by design and tend to be less common and predictably more expensive in the antiques market.

The Cordon style of glass is among the rarest of absinthe glassware, and easily recognized by the tubular ridge that encircles the smooth glass near the bottom, which serves as a dose line. This type of absinthe glass was an uncommon pattern that appeared to disappear around the time of the ban. Not many are around today.

The Reservoir glasses represent a style that possesses a distinct bulb-shaped well in the bottom of the glass, in which the green liquor is plainly visible prior to adding water. Reservoir glasses are stemmed types that may be faceted or smooth, and are typically styled like either an Egg glass or a Coupe. Because of the attractive reservoir feature,

Opposite top: A uranium Swirl glass

Opposite bottom: A Junod-branded carafe for dripping water in preparing an absinthe – many bar carafes displayed product names and were usually supplied free to the bar by the distillery.

Above left: An etched Cordon glass; an etched Egg glass, and an etched Reservoir glass

Above right: An absinthe poster from Jules Pernod in the south of France depicts two innocent figures in stylish historical dress.

Right: These rare absinthe glasses showcase a variety of artistic designs and features. Most were made by hand-blowing molten glass into a mold.

Opposite: An assortment of antique absinthe spoons

these glasses tend to bring elevated prices compared to simpler designs.

Perhaps the most desirable pattern of absinthe glass is the Pontarlier type, which is a stubby stemmed glass with an ornately faceted reservoir and cup. These are among the most desirable and least common of all antique absinthe glasses, and are priced accordingly.

On a rare occasion, a glass with an absinthe advertisement may surface, which instantly renders it particularly desirable among collectors. Similarly, a rare occasion may also yield an absinthe glass blown in ouraline – the eerie green glass sometimes called "Vaseline" or "uranium" glass that fluoresces under ultraviolet light. When these are found, they are most commonly of the Swirl pattern.

French glassblowers' catalogs from the period survive today, and the various patterns of absinthe glassware are therefore well documented. Despite this, many glasses offered as absinthe glasses on the open market are post-ban items (e.g., pastis glasses), not of French manufacture, and/or have nothing to do with absinthe.

Once upon a time, absinthe glasses were sold simply as old bistro ware, their historical use not formally identified and recognized until Marie-Claude Delahaye published *L'absinthe: Histoire de la fée verte* (1983). Demand and prices have increased steadily since that time, with the most common patterns now appearing for well under $50, while the cleanest examples of the most rare and desirable glasses have easily brought several hundred dollars.

Spoons (*Les Cuilleres*)

There is no single object more uniquely associated with the famous green elixir than the absinthe spoon. This specially designed spoon was an optional, albeit frequently used implement that served the sole purpose of further satisfying those with a sweet tooth, and accomplishing as much in style. As absinthe is an herbal, dry spirit with a slightly sweet taste, many French patrons found the drink further to their liking upon adding a lump of sugar atop the spoon and trickling ice water through it.

Absinthe spoons were produced in many different shapes and styles, of various materials and methods of manufacture (e.g., stamped vs. cast). The feature these spoons share in common is the decorative openings by which the water drips through the sugar cube into the absinthe. The most popular design consists of a trowel-shaped spoon with numerous holes of various shapes. These spoons are often referred to by the pattern of the perforations, such as *Les Pipes* (pipes), *Les Flèches* (arrows), *Les Étoiles* (stars), *Les Trèfles* (clovers or clubs), *Les Croix* (crosses), *Les Cercles* (circles), *Les Carrés* (squares or diamonds), *Les Ronds* (round), and *Les Fleurs* (flowers).

Although one might expect such intricate items to be produced from precious metals such as sterling silver, absinthe spoons were commonly made from silver-plated base metals or durable, inexpensive alloys. As expected, the heavier cast spoons are regarded as superior quality to the stamped pieces. One common quality among virtually all absinthe spoons is that, like old coins, they show some degree of wear. In some cases, the silver plating has worn away, exposing a brassy base.

Occasionally, a spoon of unusual design or shape surfaces, which makes identification as an absinthe spoon suspect. Often, spoons for culinary uses are mistaken for absinthe spoons. And predictably, the popularity of antique absinthe spoons in recent years has spawned a cottage industry of fakes. This is ostensibly because prices for original absinthe spoons can be considerable, depending upon type and condition. Fortunately, reproductions of many different antique absinthe spoons are of good quality and readily available, so one

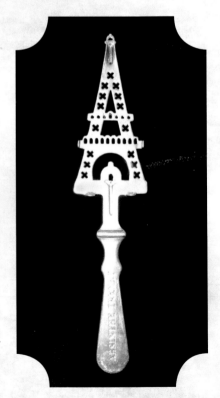

need not be a hard-core collector to enjoy the more valuable styles for everyday use.

Many of the most common original, stamped metal spoons can be had for $25 or less, with some of the more desirable cast types bringing somewhat more. Meanwhile, the upper echelon is reserved for the rare, ornate *Le Tour Eiffel*, *Coquille Saint Jacques*, *La Feuille d'Absinthe*, and *Absinthe Joanne* spoons, with some of the cleanest examples of these originals having been sold amongst avid collectors to the tune of several thousand dollars.

Fountains (*Les Fontaines*)

Whereas most cafés and bistros had water carafes available to prepare absinthe, some of the more up-scale establishments had absinthe fountains. An absinthe fountain makes a statement as the most elegant and luxurious accoutrement associated with absinthe service. Basically, an absinthe fountain is a glorified water dispenser that sits atop the bar, or is placed at the center of a round table.

A carafe depends on some degree of coordination to ensure a steady drip of water – a task that tends to become more challenging after the first couple of drinks. A fountain on the other hand is unique in

Opposite: Monogrammed absinthe spoon handles; two rare, long-handled "tea" spoons that were used to stir residue sugar into the drink

Opposite inset: An absinthe spoon in the shape of the Eiffel Tower

Right: This French six-spigot absinthe fountain is of the typical modular pattern that even includes an asbestos filter to remove particulates.

over by inebriated elbows and have not survived. Some are dented, have cracked glass, and/or leaky robinettes as a result of years of service and many more of storage. It should be noted that the same styles of fountains persisted well into the post-ban era, with many being pastis fountains, often falsely offered as absinthe-era fountains. One differentiating feature is typically the tiny handle of the robinettes — those on absinthe fountains typically have a rounded clover-like profile, while those on post-ban fountains tend to be narrow and rectangular in shape. The difference in price is usually significant, with genuine absinthe fountains carrying higher price tags.

Some fountain globes were etched with names of absinthe producers, such as the Terminus Bienfaisante fountain with rooster lid, which is perhaps the most desirable. Others include those branded as Legler Pernod, Junod, and Bailly. Some fountains etched with advertisements may reflect modern alterations to artificially increase their value. Again, such items are deserving of the utmost expert scrutiny, particularly since prices for genuine absinthe fountains in good condition can exceed $1,000. Fortunately for the noncollector, convincing reproductions can be obtained and are completely functional and practical for contemporary use.

Genuine absinthe fountains that are complete, with matching original components, and in good functional condition, can bring anywhere from $1,000 for more common patterns, to several thousand dollars for the rarer branded items. Post-ban anise and pastis fountains, while also visually appealing and functionally identical, bring considerably less.

that it allows the patron to set the pace of the water drip while providing a hands-free means of completing the drink to perfection.

More expensive than carafes, absinthe fountains consisted of a metal lamp stand topped with a glass globe to which several *robinettes* (spigots) were attached. Fountains were usually fitted with two, four, or even six robinettes, with the six-robinette version being the most commonly encountered. Complete original fountains include a metal cap that is tipped with a decorative acorn, pine bud, or rooster.

Absinthe fountains were used exclusively by patrons, and tended to be somewhat top-heavy when filled with water. Predictably, many were knocked

Carafes

Unlike absinthe fountains, water carafes were used extensively and produced in great numbers, and many have survived the passage of time, despite being subjected to the questionable grip of absinthe drinkers. Most carafes are of relatively simple design. Many are etched or painted with advertising, with some images being multicolored facsimiles of an advertising poster. Some consist of a two-piece metal and glass design that facilitates refilling with ice. Others are ceramic and sculpted in assorted shapes.

As with fountains, a water carafe isn't necessarily a pre-ban item unless it can be positively identified as such, and like fountains, some have been adorned with a bit of recently etched fakery to inflate their value, which may range anywhere from $50 to several hundred dollars. Fortunately again for the practical minded, convincing reproductions exist and are readily available.

Water carafes that can be verified as originating from the absinthe era may range anywhere from $50 for the simpler, more common patterns to several hundred dollars for the rarer branded types when in fine condition.

Opposite: A pre-ban absinthe fountain. Complete fountains like these are difficult to find intact as most have succumbed to the fate of breakage of the glass globe, an arm, or a spout.

Left: A uranium glass carafe, a clear cut glass carafe with a topper, and an Absinthe Junod glass carafe

Spoon Vases (*Les Troncs*)

It was always left up to patrons to prepare their absinthes to their individual preferences, and some preferred it with sugar, some without. For the former, that was accomplished via the absinthe spoon. And where would one find an absinthe spoon? Typically, a bar kept absinthe spoons in a metal vase referred to as a *tronc* (trunk), which was kept in plain sight for easy access. Genuine troncs are often elegant, albeit sturdy items, and sized with absinthe spoons in mind. One type is even constructed with a removable inner cup to make collecting the spoons for washing easier.

Again, an experienced eye is recommended when differentiating a genuine tronc from a spittoon or flower vase. For those interested in something relatively inexpensive and practical, good quality reproductions exist. Complete original examples of spoon vases in excellent condition can bring anywhere from $100 to several hundred dollars, especially for the rarer, more desirable patterns when complete, undamaged, and not excessively oxidized.

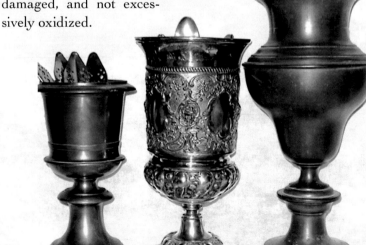

Sugar Dishes

Another café and bistro item that was conspicuously placed for the benefit of absintheurs was the *coupe á sucre* (sugar cup). These silvery dishes consisted of a pedestal and shallow bowl to hold rectangular sugar tablets. They were not uniquely associated with absinthe, but could be used to hold sugar to sweeten any beverage. Some dishes are stamped by their producers. They range in size from those that hold but a few cubes to ones suitable for a large entourage of absintheurs. Again for the budget conscious, good quality reproductions are available.

Prices for original metal sugar dishes usually range from $50 to $150 when in good condition, without dings, excessive wear, or oxidation.

Saucers

When served absinthe or any other beverage, café patrons received along with it a special ceramic saucer. These saucers were painted with various prices and came in different colors. The price on the saucer made collecting for the bill a simple matter for waitstaff and patrons alike. Café saucers were often accented with bright colors, some with gold rims, and like many ceramic and porcelain items, the name of the manufacturer was often stamped on the underside.

Opposite: Heavy spoon holders (tronc de comptoirs) in both plain and ornate patterns

Above: Metal sugar dishes and a collection of porcelain saucers with prices in francs/centimes

Ceramic saucers of this type were used both before and following the ban. As the typical price of a glass of absinthe was typically well under a franc, the lesser denominations are regarded as more likely to be pre-ban and possibly associated with absinthe. Like many other absinthe antiques, this style of saucer has been reproduced for the sake of practicality.

Original ceramic saucers have always been popular antique items, particularly when in excellent original condition and free of chips or other disappointments. Original saucers can be expected to range from $25 to $75 depending upon condition and rarity.

Topettes

Café and bistro patrons didn't always order absinthe by the glass. Establishments often made provision for purchasing multiple shots at a time via the use of a small glass bottle referred to as a topette.

A topette is a glass bottle of an inverted conical shape with numerous bulging ripples in the glass, or etched glass with volumetric graduations. Either of these features allows one to pour measured doses among several persons. Topettes were usually sized to contain anywhere from four to twelve drinks' worth of liquor, which comes in handy for a table where patrons are drinking the same thing.

Perhaps the most attractive topettes are those etched with the word *absinthe* in the glass, although such etchings can be faked. Most original topettes are clear, with fewer in color, usually either amber

Left: This pre-ban topette features dose marks that appear to be wheel-engraved into the glass. Each line and number tallies the doses of absinthe, usually around 1 ounce (approximately 30 ml) each.

Below: A Duchesses match striker

Opposite: These antique match strikers sat conveniently at the center of café tables, where they colorfully proclaimed their individual brands.

or green glass. All were originally fitted with a glass *bouchon* (stopper), which if missing reduces the value accordingly. Many items sold as topettes were actually intended for other uses (e.g., olive oil).

Original topettes that convincingly represent the type associated with bar service can usually be found priced anywhere from $50 to several hundred dollars, depending upon style, size, and condition.

Match Strikers (*Pyrogènes*)

While not directly associated with imbibing absinthe, *pyrogènes* nonetheless were ubiquitous objects found atop the marble café tables, providing a convenient repository of matchsticks for those who smoked pipes or cigars while drinking – and many did.

Pyrogènes most often consisted of small glazed ceramic vases that held matchsticks, usually with sloped sides that featured a rough surface with which

to strike a match. Some were crafted from metal, but these are not as attractive to collectors. Sometimes *pyrogènes* were adorned with conspicuous advertisements for various spirits and liqueurs, which tend to be more desirable. Of these, perhaps the Royer Hutin *pyrogène* is the most common, while those advertising Absinthe Mugnier, Absinthe Dutruc, and Cusenier Absinthe Oxygénée are among the most desirable, and therefore the most expensive.

Due to the elevated price of more desirable antique *pyrogènes*, modern fakes abound, so *caveat emptor*. Fortunately again, more desirable patterns have been reproduced for the benefit of those who wish to re-create an authentically styled café table without breaking the bank or worrying about buying a fake. Original *pyrogènes* devoid of chips and other damage can be had for under $100 for the more basic patterns. For those featuring absinthe advertisements with crisp colors and devoid of excessive crazing can bring anywhere from several hundred to well over $1,000, depending upon the brand advertised, rarity, and overall condition.

Absinthe Ducros Fils, 1901

This famous poster for Absinthe Ducros Fils, showing an exuberant lady in red brandishing an absinthe bottle, is by Leonetto Cappiello, one of the acknowledged masters of the poster. An Italian artist who lived in Paris, Cappiello has been hailed as "the father of modern advertising" because of his innovation in poster design – he was the first to use bold figures amid dark backgrounds.

Absinthe Advertised

The age of Impressionism also brought with it an age of colorful advertisements that exhibited the new style of art. New printing techniques made possible mass-produced color artwork the likes of which had never been seen. These artful ads began appearing in every nook and cranny within public view. Nowhere was this more conspicuous than in the large, full-color bills that were posted along the boulevards of Paris.

Lithographic Poster Art

The key invention that made possible the new age of color poster art took place in 1796, when a German named Alois Senefelder invented a method of printing that would become known as lithography. In this process, the ink is carried upon a flat surface rather than raised edges. Originally this was accomplished by the relatively primitive limestone and crayon method, but it later evolved into the use of zinc plates and a very fine distribution of colored inks. Frenchman

Jules Chéret developed considerable expertise with the technique in the mid-nineteenth century, using it to design more than a thousand advertising posters. So prevalent were Chéret's posters that he is widely regarded as the father of poster art. Of course, the ability to print color posters is half the equation, the other half being the artwork itself. Fortunately, Parisian society held numerous accomplished artists who stepped up to the task. Chéret's own stable included experts such as Théophile Alexandre Steinlen, Eugène Grasset, Pierre Bonnard, Adolphe Leon Willette, Jean-Louis Forain, and most notably, Henri de Toulouse-Lautrec.

The golden age of the promotional poster was in sync with the Belle Époque, and seductive advertisements were used to portray the venues and wares they represented as fashionable. The presentation of voluptuous female subjects in liquor ads was particularly adventurous, as it skirted the edge of propriety by illustrating women drinking these products in conspicuous attempts to capture the attention of men. The women who graced these images were not limited to figments of the imagination, but included celebrities of the day such Sarah Bernhardt, Yvette Guilbert, Eugénie Buffet, Camille Stefani, Jane Avril, La Goulue, and Loie Fuller, all of whom are immortalized in classic Belle Époque advertisements.

Original advertisement posters from the Belle Époque encompass a wide range of products and services, and have brought sales ranging anywhere from a pittance to hundreds of thousands of dollars. Naturally, those by Toulouse-Lautrec have proven to be particularly valuable. Many of the more popular posters, including absinthe-related posters, have been reproduced as giclées, which is a bit more practical for decorative purposes.

Fortunately for the collector of absinthe memorabilia, original absinthe advertising posters can be found in a presentable condition on rare occasion. When opportunity arises, one can expect to shell out anywhere from $15 to $15,000, depending upon size, rarity, original artist, condition, and the notability of the brand advertised.

Above: This colorized postcard depicts a woman stirring sugar into her absinthe. The two empty bottles at her feet humorously suggest this is not her first glass.

Right: This rare buvard on pastel blue/gray blotting paper advertises Abrial Absinthe Blanche – a clear absinthe. The woman is commenting that it is her preference.

Opposite: This print depicts a little boy drinking absinthe outside a café. The bottom caption reads: "Dans le Doubs absinthe-toi," which in English means, "When in Doubs, drink absinthe." The Doubs region is regarded as the historical center of absinthe production in France.

Buvards

Some absinthe advertisements were made as a *buvard* (blotting paper). This was used to quickly blot excess ink by pressing it against a freshly written letter or signature. Although in use for some time, it wasn't until the mid-nineteenth century that these became popularized as advertising tools.

The advertisements imprinted on *buvards* ranged from simple monochromatic images to striking full-color works, some advertising popular brands of absinthe, such as Edouard Pernod. *Buvards* are an interesting artifact of absinthiana, although they have not been the focus of determined collectors. As such, unused *buvards* often appear in the antiquities market for very reasonable prices.

Caution to the Buyer

Do not assume that the brown-tinted paper of a document or postcard is evidence of the item's antiquity. In fact, this "foxing" can be due to the presence of a brown fungal growth. Not only can this mislead the inexperienced collector, but it also may present a danger to any nearby paper collection. While some light mold can be brushed off, affected items should be stored separately in sealed bags to prevent the possibility of spreading to the entire collection.

Cartons

The carton was a stiff piece of paperboard or enameled metal that was printed and often embossed with an advertisement. Heavier and more durable than a poster, these were intended to be affixed to a café or bistro wall. Many aperitif wines, liqueurs, and spirits were advertised on cartons, including popular tipples such as Byrrh, Suze, Amer Picon, and various brands of absinthe. Although they occasionally turn up in continental flea markets, many survivors are not in very good condition.

Dans le Doubs absinthe-toi

Advertising cartons do surface from time to time, although most are discolored from years of exposure to smoke and/or water. Many have seen better days, but some have survived in aged, but presentable condition. Pricing for cartons varies widely, depending upon size, brand advertised, and condition.

Postcards

One category of item that has attracted the interest of many a collector is the classic French *carte postale* (postcard). Long before the advent of email and social media, postcards were printed with a variety of humorous and picturesque images as well as advertisements. Many cards carried satirical illustrations, some of these pertaining to the evils of absinthe, which are especially desirable.

The Pernod Fils distillery printed sets of twenty-eight numbered postcards that featured black-and-white photographs of the distillery and the various steps of absinthe production. Included are images of absinthe plants, women working the bottling line, laborers loading product onto vehicles, and even an image of the distillery burning down in 1901. Pernod also issued full-color cards, but these are post-ban items.

Some cards were printed in sets containing several cards that were intended to be sent in numbered sequence, the end result being a short story. One notable example is a six-card set with photographs depicting a child who takes advantage of his grandfather's absence by reading the newspaper, preparing an absinthe, and smoking a cigar. It was neither improper nor uncommon to employ the services of children in promoting alcohol-related postcard humor. Other sequential sets illustrated the step-by-step art of preparing an absinthe, each set representing the male or female point of view, respectively.

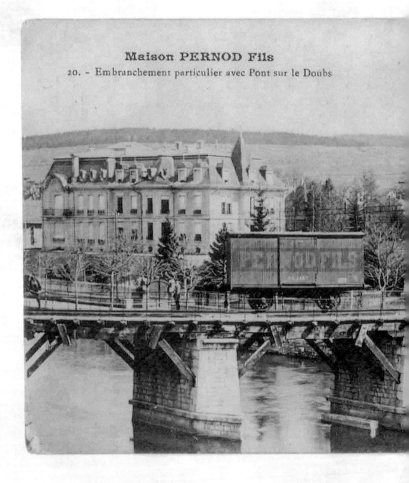

Maison PERNOD Fils
20. – Embranchement particulier avec Pont sur le Doubs

Postcards that carry full-color advertisements for absinthe often fetch less than $100, while black-and-white versions often fall in the $50 to $60 range. Cards that are part of a numbered series pertaining to absinthe are usually offered anywhere from $30 to $150, depending on rarity and condition.

Left: This Pernod Fils postcard features a photo of the huge Pontarlier distillery.

Right: An early twentieth-century photograph of three men drinking Pernod Fils absinthe. At the time, Pernod Fils was the largest producer and regarded as a cornerstone of quality.

Below: This postcard advertises Cusenier's Oxygénée Absinthe Verte as the clear winner and record holder.

6

ABSINTHE
and the CRAFT
COCKTAIL REVIVAL

The first part of the twenty-first century was a turbulent period in the world of absinthe. On the one hand, modern science was gaining leverage in undoing the old, unfounded prejudices that virtually eradicated the once popular spirit. On the other hand, the vast majority of products being sold as absinthe amounted to nothing but artificially colored flavored vodkas with inflated price tags and empty promises, aimed at exploiting consumer ignorance at considerable profit. This combination of circumstances had the net effect of generating interest in while simultaneously damaging the credibility of the spirit. Many consumers who ended up with a bottle of overpriced rubbish chose not to be taken a second time. Perhaps nowhere was this more evident than in the UK, where in a matter of a few short years absinthe was reduced to a flaming shot favored by hooligans aiming to get drunk. The source of the problem was universal – no country had ever recognized a legal definition for the spirit. By 2004, Europe was awash in cheap absinthes originating from the Czech Republic, Spain, Germany, and even France, many being sold under the false premise of delivering drug-like effects.

There were, however, bright spots amidst the chaos that troubled the market. The internet had given rise to online forums and discussion groups frequented by hard-core absinthe connoisseurs, who shared experiences in tasting antique absinthes and evaluating new ones. It is this congregation of

Opposite: This Absinthe Parisienne ad by P. Gélis-Didot and Louis Malteste (1894) highlights an illustrated version of Molière's Doctor Diafoirus from Le Malade Ímaginaire.

Absinthe Festival (June) in the Val-de-Travers, Switzerland, where a multitude of clandestine Swiss absinthes could be imbibed and traded, and the Absinthiades Festival (October) in Pontarlier, France, a focal point for the absinthe antiques trade.

And while it often seemed that the virtues of legitimate absinthes would remain reserved for a limited group of individuals dedicated to the preservation of the spirit, little by little, light was becoming visible at the end of the tunnel. By 2004, a few intrepid Americans and Brits had enlisted the cooperation of the French Combier and Emile Pernot distilleries pursuant to the development and commercial release of authentic French absinthes. In 2005, the repeal of the Swiss ban and simultaneous implementation of a strict legal definition had the effect of legitimizing a clutch of clandestine distillers, making commercially available their artisanally distilled Swiss La Bleue style of absinthes. And finally, 2007 yielded the repeal of the long-standing US ban, which opened a substantial new market, along with simultaneous consumer education efforts to demonstrate that the debacle of phony absinthes plaguing Europe did not migrate to American shores.

At the time the US Alcohol and Tobacco Tax and Trade Bureau lifted its ban on absinthe, a new wave was stirring in the undercurrents of the cocktail world. This trend would follow in the wake of the food revolution that had taken root in the early 1990s, which brought bold new flavors and cuisines to the masses. By 2000, this revival had completely overhauled the restaurant scene in cities around

enthusiasts who hailed from various nations around the globe that deserves perhaps the most credit for identifying credible products, vilifying the imposters, and making available a great deal of reliable information and active discussion to everyone capable of using a search engine. Furthermore, many of these absinthe cognoscenti convened annually at the only two absinthe festivals on earth – the Boveresse

the globe, with London being a particularly notable example. By the first decade of the twenty-first century, it had become clear that the renaissance that catered to foodies around the world was crossing over into the world of drinks.

The first known use of the term *cocktail* appears in a magazine from 1803, and is described as being made from any spirit, bitters, sugar, and water. This simplistic formula would eventually revolutionize the way Western society imbibes adult beverages. By the mid-nineteenth century, the cocktail phenomenon had become established in North America, and was exerting measurable influence back in England. Perhaps the standard-bearer

Opposite: This image juxtaposes one of the antique absinthe fountains of the Old Absinthe House in New Orleans against a background of modern frozen drink machines in an adjacent property. Fortunately, the old fountains have since been returned to their original locations.

Below: (Author) T.A. Breaux working the antique Renaud pot stills at Combier in France.

of the fancy cocktail was the *Sazerac*, which was originally crafted from cognac, absinthe, Peychaud's bitters, and sugar, then stirred with ice and strained. As the cocktail trend swept through cosmopolitan American cities, books began to appear in print, beginning in 1862 with *Jerry Thomas's Bartender's Guide: How to Mix Drinks*, Harry Johnson's *Bartender's Manual* in 1882, and wonderful repositories of fancy cocktails, such as C.F. Lawlor's *The Mixicologist* (1895) and William Schmidt's *The Flowing Bowl — What and When to Drink* (1892). These books all gave tribute to the delicious cocktails that had become most fashionable in civilized locales. And one ingredient they all employed in their artistic creations is none other than the perfumed green elixir that hailed from France and Switzerland – absinthe.

The distinctly American wave of fancy drinks, artfully mixed from wholesome spirits, aromatized wines, and liqueurs, and adorned with fresh fruits, was in full swing by 1900. But the clouds of temperance grew even darker on American shores than in Europe, during the United States's failed experiment known as Prohibition. In a span of thirteen years, American society had swept away its cocktail culture, creating nothing in its wake aside from smugglers, an underworld of nefarious gangsters, and millions of lawbreaking citizens. What the French and Swiss bans had done for absinthe, Prohibition had done for the American cocktail. It was amidst this dark period that US bartender Harry Craddock traveled to London to continue his craft in the American Bar of the Savoy Hotel. In 1930, he published what is regarded by many as the premier compilation of fancy cocktails of the era, *The Savoy Cocktail Book*. In this tome are more than one hundred cocktails that call for absinthe, which showcased absinthe's versatility as Belle Époque French society had never known it.

Following the Second World War, the postwar industrialization of historically artisanal spirits, and the invention of the juice gun, by 1990 the American

cocktail had reached the bottom of the barrel. The word *cocktail* had come to represent mostly sugary novelties mixed from cheap cordials aimed at dazzling consumers with an array of artificial rainbow colors and flavors. Such would have been the doomed course of the cocktail if it were not for but a

Opposite: This vintage Absinthe Royer-Hutin carpet, or tapis de carte, was used for table games in bars.

Opposite inset: A Coquille Saint Jacques–style grille

Right: This clever advertising distraction from Terminus made it convenient to drip water into one's glass while the embossed verbiage extols the virtues of the brand.

classic cocktail and absinthe coincided. As of 2007, once again, those one hundred-plus cocktails described by Craddock in 1930 that called for absinthe could be properly re-created not only in the States but around the world, and by 2016, the rebirth of the classic cocktail had become firmly established as a global trend.

Back in 1895, C.F. Lawlor noted in *The Mixicologist* that the flavor of many cocktails is improved with a few drops of absinthe. In his guidebook *The Gentleman's Companion* (1939), Charles Baker adds that absinthe is an essential for every well-stocked bar. Even Don the Beachcomber is reported to have used absinthe as a secret ingredient in the tiki drinks he made famous. These observations are as true today as they were during the last two centuries, as cocktail chefs around the world have rediscovered absinthe. Just as learning the classic dishes of French cuisine provides a healthy perspective for creating new delicacies, learning the form and function of classic cocktails provides a knowledge base from which to create modern classics. And where the classics are concerned, it seems that absinthe was used in abundance for cocktails deemed to be "eye openers," such as the famous Corpse Reviver #2 and Absinthe Frappé. Otherwise, absinthe was used mostly in smaller amounts to bolster the flavor of once-popular aromatized wines, aperitifs, strong spirits, and liqueurs, yielding fashionable cocktails such as the Angelus and Morning Glory Fizz. Whether one is re-creating the classics or creating new classics, the key to success in mixing a delicious cocktail is balance.

mere handful of individuals, most notably esteemed New York cocktail king Dale DeGroff, who upheld a standard of excellence not seen since the days before Prohibition. With the catalyst of the food revolution in full swing, the cocktail's evolution began a gradual change in course akin to that of the *Titanic*, but unlike the ill-fated steamer, it managed to dodge the iceberg of obscurity and return to relevance by the first decade of the twenty-first century. How serendipitous it was that the renaissance of both the

COCKTAILS

Pre-Prohibition Classics

Absinthe Special Cocktail

The Savoy Cocktail Book, Harry Craddock, 1930

> 1 dash Angostura bitters
> 1 dash orange bitters
> $^2/_3$ absinthe
> $^1/_6$ gin
> $^1/_6$ gomme syrup
>
> Shake well, strain into cocktail glass.

Angelus

The Flowing Bowl, William Schmidt, 1892

> 1 dash gum syrup
> 2 dashes orange bitters
> 2 dashes curaçao
> 1 dash absinthe
> a little vino (Italian) vermouth
> 1 pony Old Tom Gin
>
> Stir well and strain into a fancy glass.

Right: While this pre-ban absinthe bottle label boasts the national shield of Switzerland, many French distilleries adopted this emblem to confirm the product was crafted by the Swiss method, which meant that it was distilled from whole botanicals and was not a cheap, industrial imitation.

Corpse Reviver #2

The Savoy Cocktail Book, Harry Craddock, 1930

> 1 oz. gin
> 1 oz. Cointreau
> 1 oz. Lillet Blanc
> 1 oz. fresh lemon juice
> 1 dash absinthe
>
> Shake all ingredients with ice, strain into a chilled cocktail glass, and garnish with orange peel.

Death in the Afternoon

So Red the Nose or – Breath in the Afternoon,
Sterling North and Carl Kroch, 1935

1 oz. absinthe
Champagne

Pour absinthe into a champagne coupe or flute. Add iced champagne until it attains the proper opalescence.

Eye Opener

Harry Johnson's Bartender's Manual,
Harry Johnson, 1882

¾ glass full of finely shaved ice
1 egg white
¾ wine glass absinthe
¼ wine glass whiskey, if required, Old Tom Gin or Scotch whiskey; shake well with a shaker

Strain into a medium-sized fizz glass, fill with carbonic water, put a little fruit in the glass, and serve.

Brunelle Cocktail

The Savoy Cocktail Book, Harry Craddock, 1930

¼ absinthe
½ tablespoon sugar
¾ lemon juice

Shake well and strain into cocktail glass.

Frappé

T.A. Breaux

1 oz. absinthe
½ oz. simple syrup
6–8 fresh mint leaves (optional)
1 oz. soda water

Muddle 6–8 mint leaves and simple syrup in a tall glass. Add crushed ice, pour in absinthe, cover with a cocktail shaker, and shake vigorously. Top with soda water. Alternatively, instead of the mint, a piece of any fruit can be added into the cocktail shaker.

French Absinthe Drip

T.A. Breaux

1½ oz. absinthe
1 lump sugar (optional)
Iced water

Pour absinthe into suitable cocktail glass. Drip iced water (over sugar) into glass until absinthe becomes completely cloudy. Taste. Add more water if desired.

Monkey Gland Cocktail

The Savoy Cocktail Book, Harry Craddock, 1930

>3 dashes absinthe
>
>2 dashes grenadine
>
>$1/3$ orange juice
>
>$2/3$ dry gin

Shake well, strain into cocktail glass.

Morning Glory Fizz

The Savoy Cocktail Book, Harry Craddock, 1930

>1 dash lemon or 2 dashes lime juice
>
>½ tablespoon powdered sugar
>
>1 egg white
>
>2 dashes absinthe
>
>1 glass Scotch whiskey

Shake well, strain into long timber, and fill with soda water.

Stars Fell on Alabama

So Red the Nose or – Breath in the Afternoon, Sterling North and Carl Kroch, 1935

>1 dash Peychaud's Bitters
>
>1 dash Angostura bitters
>
>1 dash orange flower water
>
>1 lump sugar
>
>6 drops absinthe
>
>1 jigger old Alabama corn whiskey

Ice and stir briskly.

Sazerac

T.A. Breaux

>2 oz. rye whiskey
>
>¼ oz. absinthe
>
>¼ oz. Peychaud's Bitters
>
>Simple syrup
>
>Lemon peel

Add rye whiskey, absinthe, bitters, and simple syrup to a bar glass and stir vigorously over ice. Enough syrup should be added such that the result is just slightly sweet. Strain into a suitable cocktail glass and garnish with a twist of lemon peel.

Modern Classics

Bloody Fairy

1 oz. absinthe
5–6 oz. Bloody Mary mix
Worcestershire sauce
Horseradish

Combine all into a suitable glass and serve with the usual garnishes.

Ginger Mint Julep

T.A. Breaux

1¼ oz. absinthe
½ oz. ginger liqueur
6–8 mint leaves
Soda water

Muddle mint in bottom of glass and fill with ice. In a cocktail shaker, add ice, absinthe, and ginger liqueur. Shake vigorously and strain into glass. Add splash of soda water.

Green Beast

www.pernodabsinthe.com

1 oz. absinthe
1 oz. fresh lime juice
1 oz. simple syrup
4 oz. water

Add all the ingredients to a collins glass filled with ice. Garnish with cucumber slices and stir.

St. Germainiac

T.A. Breaux

1¼ oz. elderflower liqueur
¼ oz. absinthe
7 dashes Angostura bitters
Ginger ale
Orange slice

Add elderflower liqueur, absinthe, and bitters to bar glass and stir vigorously with ice. Strain into cocktail glass, top with ginger ale, and garnish with orange slice.

Opposite: A topette was an ingenious bottle used to serve as well as measure. Each curve measured a dose of absinthe, which was then calculated visually for the bill.

RECIPES

Not to be overshadowed by the realm of fancy drinks, absinthe has also enjoyed a long-standing history as a secret ingredient in the culinary world. Unlike one-dimensional, sugary anise liqueurs, a traditional absinthe contributes distinct herbal notes and nuances to savory dishes and confections alike. This was clearly evident in the nineteenth century, when a palate-cleansing course of absinthe sorbet was served to Gustave Eiffel at a posh dinner to commemorate the opening of the Eiffel Tower in 1889. Across the Atlantic in 1899, a drizzle of absinthe was the secret ingredient of the original oysters Rockefeller recipe created by Antoine's restaurant in New Orleans. And of course, there was the previously mentioned, infamous François Mitterand incident in 1983 involving a soufflé served with absinthe ice cream, which landed one Swiss chef in a heap of legal trouble.

Absinthe Beefsteak Tomatoes and Mozzarella

Ingredients:

- 2 slices red beefsteak tomatoes
- 2 slices yellow beefsteak tomatoes
- 2 slices Vidalia onions
- 3 slices fresh mozzarella
- 2 oz. pesto
- 2 oz. balsamic glaze
- 2 oz. absinthe
- Garnish of fresh basil

Method:

1. Attractively arrange alternately tomatoes, onions, and mozzarella on a plate. Top with pesto in a line down the middle of items.
2. Mix balsamic glaze and absinthe together and pour next to tomatoes, onion, and mozzarella.
3. Garnish with fresh basil.

Scallops, Orange, and Absinthe Butter Sauce

Ingredients (serves 4):

- 12 U-10 sea scallops
- 4 T grapeseed oil
- salt and pepper, as needed
- ½ cup orange segments
- garnish of tarragon leaves

Method:

1. Dry the scallops with a paper towel and season with salt and pepper.
2. Heat a sauté pan on high heat until hot.
3. Add the grapeseed oil to the pan and wait for a light smoke.
4. Add the scallops to the pan and cook 4–5 minutes on each side until just cooked through.
5. Serve with the orange segments to the side and a drizzle of the Absinthe butter sauce. Garnish with tarragon leaves.

Absinthe Butter Sauce

Ingredients:

- 2 T unsalted butter
- 1 T minced shallots
- 1 sprig thyme
- 1 T tarragon, chopped
- 1 T champagne vinegar
- 4 T absinthe
- 4 T heavy cream
- 10 oz. butter, cubed, at room temperature
- salt and pepper to taste

Method:

1. In a small sauce pot, sweat the shallots and 2 T butter together over medium heat until tender.
2. Add the thyme, tarragon, champagne vinegar and absinthe and cook until reduced by half (3–4 minutes).
3. Add the cream and reduce again by half.
4. Remove from the heat and add the butter one cube at a time while slowly stirring to create an emulsification. Once the cube of butter is incorporated, add another and continue until all the butter has been added.
5. Move the pan on and off the heat if needed to keep the sauce warm, but do not heat the sauce too much, as it can separate.
6. Season with salt and pepper.
7. Strain and serve with pan-seared sea scallops and fresh orange segments.

Absinthe Mussels

Ingredients:

- ½ lb. fresh cleaned large mussels in shells (rinsed)
- 1 oz. fresh chopped basil
- 4 oz. plum tomato strips (canned pomodoro)
- 1 oz. julienne fresh leeks
- 2 oz. garlic butter
- 2 oz. fresh chopped shallots
- 4 oz. clam juice
- 2 oz. absinthe
- Garnish of fresh chopped Italian parsley
- 2 ea. grilled baguette bread, thick slices
- Season to taste with salt and pepper

Method:

1. Combine all ingredients except bread in heavy saucepan or pot, and bring to boil until mussels are opened and cooked. Season to taste.
2. Garnish with parsley and serve in a serving bowl with grilled warm baguette bread.

Dauphinoise Potatoes

Ingredients: (yields one 2" hotel pan)

- ¾ hotel pan 2" full of sliced, peeled baker potatoes
- 1 qt. heavy cream
- 1 lb. grated Parmesan cheese
- 1 oz. chopped fine garlic
- 4 oz. shredded Parmesan cheese
- 3 oz. clarified butter
- 3 oz. absinthe
- Season to taste with kosher salt and white pepper

Method:

1. Mix and layer all ingredients except shredded cheese and clarified butter in hotel pan, keeping flat.
2. Lightly press down potato mixture in pan to ensure all is flat. Evenly lace top with clarified butter and sprinkle top with shredded cheese.
3. Cover with sheet pan paper and foil and tightly seal.
4. Bake in preheated 375° oven for approx. 35–40 minutes, remove paper and foil cover, and bake an additional 20–25 minutes until knife-tender and golden brown.
5. Let rest and cut in squares and serve.

Absinthe Fettuccine Lobster Thermidor

Ingredients: (2 servings)

- 16 oz. precooked fettuccine pasta
- 12 oz. cooked fresh lobster meat (large diced)
- 8 oz. fresh chanterelle mushrooms
- 2 oz. fresh butter
- 1½ oz. chopped tarragon
- 2 oz. prepared mustard
- 12 oz. preheated lobster sauce (good lobster bisque)
- 3 oz. fresh chopped chives
- 2 oz. cognac
- 2 oz. absinthe
- Season to taste with salt and pepper
- Garnish of fresh basil

Method:

1. Lightly heat up sauté skillet with butter, lobster, and mushrooms, and sauté gently, heating thoroughly.
2. Deglaze with cognac and absinthe and flambé.
3. Add mustard, tarragon, and lobster sauce and toss gently.
4. Add pasta and toss again, add fresh chives, and season to taste with salt and pepper.
5. Garnish with fresh basil and serve hot immediately.

Absinthe Cioppino

Ingredients:
(1 serving)

- 2 ea. jumbo sea scallops, U-10
- 3 ea. shrimp, U 13–15
- 4 ea. mussels
- 1 ea. 4 oz. lobster tail, split in half lengthwise
- 4 ea. littleneck clams
- 8 oz. tomato garlic broth with absinthe
- 3 oz. appropriate vegetable garnish (fennel, leeks, garlic, tomatoes, and onions)
- 3 oz. cooked linguine pasta
- Garnish of fresh fennel fern

Heat all ingredients until all seafood is cooked, and finish with cooked pasta.

Absinthe Cioppino Broth

Ingredients:
(yields approx. 1½ gallons)

- 1 gal. fish stock
- 10 oz. chopped fresh tomato concasse
- 8 oz. chopped fine garlic
- 8 oz. julienne leeks
- 8 oz. fresh fennel, chopped brunoise
- 6 oz. julienne white onion
- 4 oz. olive oil
- 10 oz. white wine
- 8 oz. absinthe
- 4 oz. tomato puree
- 2 ea. bay leaves
- Season to taste with kosher salt and white pepper

Method:

1. Mix and add all ingredients in heavy sauce stock pot and let simmer uncovered over medium heat for 1 hour.
2. Remove bay leaves only as they can be a throat hazard.
3. Ready for service. Do not strain.

Absinthe Vegetarian Linguine

Ingredients: (1 serving)

- 8 oz. par cooked linguine
- 3 oz. fresh spinach
- 4 oz. sweet peas
- 4 ea. pear tomatoes cut in halves
- 4 oz. wild mushrooms
- 2 oz. Asiago cheese
- 4 oz. extra virgin olive oil
- 2 oz. absinthe
- Garnish of fresh basil and shaved Reggiano

Method:

1. In a large sauté pan heat olive oil. Add all vegetables and sweat until slightly tender. Add pasta, Asiago cheese, and absinthe and heat thoroughly.
2. Serve hot and garnish with Reggiano cheese and fresh basil.

Absinthe Panna Cotta

Ingredients: (8 servings)

- 1.5 cups double cream
- 1 cup whole milk
- 4 T granulated sugar
- pinch salt
- 1.5 t powdered gelatin dissolved in 2 oz. water
- 2.5 oz. absinthe
- fresh raspberries, for serving
- whipped cream, for serving

Method:

1. In a saucepot, combine the cream, milk, sugar, and salt and bring to a simmer until the sugar is dissolved.
2. Add the bloomed gelatin and stir until the gelatin has dissolved.
3. Pour in the absinthe, reserving a small splash for the whipped cream.
4. Divide the mixture into 8 small serving dishes and refrigerate until completely cool.
5. Add the remaining splash of absinthe to the whipped cream. Garnish the puddings with the prepared whipped cream and fresh raspberries.

All culinary recipes graciously provided by:

Ryan Clark
Certified Executive Chef, Author, and Food and Beverage Consultant

and

Norman Nichols II
Certified Executive Chef Vice Conseiller Culinaire/ Officier Commandeur

7

ABSINTHE
REVIEWS

In the early days of the absinthe renaissance, the absence of a proper legal definition and consumer expertise allowed profiteers to exploit buyers with bogus products. Gradually, the tide has begun to turn against this practice, thanks to bottles of pre-ban absinthe unearthed from dark wine cellars of European estates revealing their secrets, the uncovering of detailed written publications from the past, and a growing popularity of craft spirits that are more accurately representative of their historic predecessors. Additionally, the educational efforts by absinthe connoisseurs coupled with the dissemination of accurate information via the web has done much to inform the masses, which has resulted in consumers who are better educated in spirits and more discriminating when purchasing them. So influential has this movement become that several notable producers of the green spirit have vastly improved the quality and historical accuracy of their brands to better address consumer expectations.

Despite these efforts, absinthe remains a niche spirit of varying quality from a global standpoint, and the road back to a position of respectability has been fraught with challenges. Because a proper legal definition remains lacking everywhere but Switzerland, inferior brands containing sugar and dye persist, although US consumers have the advantage of more easily identifying those containing sugar and dye by scanning the label for legally required disclosures such as "Herbal Liqueur" and "Contains FD&C Yellow No. 5," respectively.

Opposite: Gentlemen toasting with absinthe. Note the branded Absinthe Junod carafe, deep sugar dish, and the popular swirled absinthe glasses.

For much of the rest of the world, it remains a matter of *caveat emptor*. On the other hand, unusually tough regulations maintained by some countries have driven up compliance costs for artisanal producers without any return benefit. Furthermore, a coup was orchestrated in 2010 by several Swiss distillers who aimed to reserve legal use of the term *absinthe* for themselves alone, which would be akin to the Belgians cornering the use of the term *beer* exclusively for Belgian products. This attempt to exclude the rest of the world drew stiff opposition. Fortunately, the effort failed.

By all credible historical accounts from treatises on distillation as well as the Belle Époque distillers themselves, and confirmed by the liquid contained within numerous sealed examples of the best brands of the spirit from before the ban, absinthe is a distilled herbal liquor, historically ranging from 45 to 75 percent (up to 150 proof) alcohol by volume. Traditional absinthe is always distilled from grand absinthe (*Artemisia absinthium*), green anise (*Pimpinella anisum*), sweet fennel (*Foeniculum vulgare* var. *dulce*), and any of many different European herbs of medicinal and/or culinary significance. Its famous green tint traditionally results from the presence of chlorophyll, extracted from an added infusion of botanicals after the distillation, although contemporary Swiss absinthes often omit this step. Its finished appearance ranges from crystal clear to any of many different shades of natural green. Where colored with hibiscus (of rare historical precedence), it takes on a rose to light-red tint. As absinthe was never a sweetened liqueur, it should never be bottled with sugar. When tasted neat, a proper absinthe yields fiery flavors of absinthium, anise, and fennel, with distinct herbaceous notes. Upon the addition of iced water, it gradually louches, through which its clarity and/or green tint gives way to a thick, creamy opaqueness, releasing a bouquet of hidden aromas and appearance that ranges from milky white to jade green.

Opposite: One of a series of three monkey-centric postcards that advertises Absinthe Junod, the second largest producer at the turn of the twentieth century.

Right top: A tiny coin/cosmetic leather purse with etched flowers surrounding the mirror. Its now-faded, stamped gold letters say, "Absinthe Quinquina Parandier, Pontarlier."

Right bottom: A bronze match striker advertising Cusenier Absinthe

La Buveuse d'Absinthe

La buveuse d'absinthe, c'est la petite
grisette du quartier latin qui ne dédaigne pas
de tremper ses lèvres roses dans la perfide
liqueur verte.
  La môme du quartier latin
  Entre fort bien chez le "Chand d'vin"
  Avec son amant en goguette.
  Holà! Troquet, deux môminettes!

While the absinthes reviewed herein represent but a fraction of what is currently available in the global market, they represent some of the most visible and significant examples at the time of this writing. This brief selection includes only brands that strictly adhere to the Swiss legal definition, which demands that the spirit is artisanally distilled from whole botanicals, delivers a flavor profile historically associated with that of absinthe, louches appropriately upon the addition of water, and is not adulterated with sugar or artificial dyes. Simply put, if a product that claims to be a traditional absinthe is flavored vodka or otherwise contains adulterants, it will not appear in this section.

The following list is in alphabetical order. Where available, the website of the producer or sole distributor has been provided for each product. Where a product is in any way connected to the writers of this book, independent reviews from credible experts have been reprinted with permission for the sake of objectivity. To obtain the familiar US proof measure of strength, simply double the indicated percent alcohol by volume (% ABV).

Additional reviews of these absinthes and many more can be found within two long-standing, non-branded repositories of unbiased, accurate information on all matters absinthe:

Wormwood Society
(www.wormwoodsociety.org)

La Fée Verte
(www.feeverte.net)

Above: This amusing postcard depicts a female absinthe drinker who is evidently a party girl from the Parisian Latin Quarter.

Opposite: A cloud of vapor emerges from the bain marie *(hot steam bath) of an antique Egrot still at Combier.*

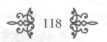

BUTTERFLY CLASSIC ABSINTHE

65% ABV
Distillerie Artemisia-Bugnon
Couvet, Switzerland
www.butterflyabsinthe.com

Butterfly Classic Absinthe represents a joint effort between American absinthe enthusiast Brian Fernald and Swiss distiller Claude-Alain Bugnon, to re-create an American brand of absinthe that was first distilled in 1902 by the P. Dempsey and Co. in Boston, Massachusetts. Originally founded by Irish immigrant Patrick Dempsey, the Dempsey Co. engaged in the business of wholesaling liquors, including two whiskeys, a gin, and an absinthe. Having sifted through the holdings of the Dempsey family, much information was recovered from old documentation about the original brand, including handwritten details of the original recipe. These findings were used to reproduce the flavor profile of the original pre-ban American Butterfly Absinthe.

Butterfly Classic Absinthe employs classic botanicals such as green anise, sweet fennel, and grand absinthe in its construction, as well as coriander, Roman wormwood, lemon balm, hyssop, and peppermint. Bottled at 65% in dark glass, Butterfly retains its attractive translucent olive tint. Louching with iced water brings about a thick glowing opacity, and seasoned palates will likely find the addition of 1½ to 2 volumes of water to be sufficient. When appropriately louched, the aroma that emanates from the glass can be described as soft, minty, and powdery. The aroma translates directly into the flavor, which expresses itself as an integrated amalgam of meadow herbs with a sweet wave of powder and mint. The initial flavor gives way to a burst of fennel that appears mid-palate, which gradually subsides to a reasonably long reprise of the soft powdery herbal notes with distinct minty accompaniment.

– T.A. Breaux

First launched in 2005, the Duplais series of absinthes is the brainchild of Markus Lyon of Freiburg, Germany, working in conjunction with the Matter-Luginbühl distillery in Kallnach, Switzerland. Having earned a distinction for producing fine-quality artisan spirits and fruit-based distilled *eaux de vie* and liqueurs, Nicole and Oliver of Matter-Luginbühl worked with Markus to produce several absinthes from this small Swiss locale, including a blanche absinthe, Mansinthe, Brevans, and several others. The distillery lies just inside the German-speaking rural meadows of western Switzerland. These absinthes are part of the Tempus Fugit Spirits US portfolio.

Duplais Swiss Absinthe Verte represents the first release of the Duplais range, is distilled using early twentieth-century copper alembic stills, and is bottled at 68% ABV in dark glass. This absinthe begins with a base of grain neutral spirits, a blend of both Pontarlier and Swiss grande absinthe, and other botanicals, which are undisclosed, but certainly include green anise, sweet fennel, and others integral to traditional absinthes. The liquid pours a golden olive tint into the glass, and yields a gentle opacity upon the addition of 2 to 2½ parts iced water, where a mild herbal aroma resembling Roman wormwood becomes evident. Upon tasting, Flavors of well-balanced absinthe, green anise, and lightly piquant fennel emerge, that progress into light-bodied herbaceous notes of coloring herbs and a slightly sweet yet savory finish.

– T.A. Breaux

DUPLAIS SWISS
ABSINTHE VERTE
68% ABV
Matter-Luginbühl
Kallnach, Switzerland
www.absinthe.de/en

JADE ESPRIT EDOUARD ABSINTHE SUPÉRIEURE

72% ABV
Jade Liqueurs
Combier Distillery
Saumur, France
www.jadeliqueurs.com

Jade Liqueurs was founded in 2000 by T.A. Breaux for the purpose of restoring integrity to a category littered with cheap imposters. By virtue of an arrangement with Franck Choisne of the historical Combier distillery in Saumur, France, Breaux began distilling in January 2004, launching Jade's first commercial release, Nouvelle-Orléans Absinthe Supérieure, in the summer of that year. In 2005, Jade launched Esprit Edouard Absinthe Supérieure, one of several releases in the Jade portfolio that Breaux reverse engineered using original bottles of the spirit as a basis. Esprit Edouard Absinthe Supérieure is a facsimile of the export-strength version of a very popular French absinthe from the end of the nineteenth century.

Jade Esprit Edouard is another attempt by Mr. Breaux to recreate a top marque from the Belle Époque.

Again using very dark glass to help protect the freshness of the product, this absinthe is bottled at 72% and is presented with a label reminiscent of the original Belle Époque brand. While pouring out a sample, one notices the color: a slightly darker shade of green compared to the 1901 version – similar to the hues of a high-quality, first-pressed olive oil. The louche builds slowly through the first volume of water then practically explodes into an invitingly thick, milky-green end result. Aromas include bracing wormwood, hyssop, and baking spices, deep and floral. The flavor follows along the same line with minty freshness, sweet anise, and a slightly dry, spicy finish. The earthy fennel also makes itself apparent, adding another layer of complexity. It is powerful, yet graceful.

– Brian Robinson

La Clandestine Absinthe Supérieure represents the first commercial bottling of former clandestine Swiss distiller Claude-Alain Bugnon. Once one of the most sought bootlegged absinthes from the historic Val-de-Travers, La Clandestine became a legitimate commercial absinthe when the Swiss ban was repealed in 2005. Bugnon practices his craft in a quiet shop located in the sleepy Swiss town of Couvet, which was home to several famous absinthe distillers more than a century ago. The relegalization of absinthe in the region of its birth has made it possible for Bugnon and several other formerly clandestine distillers to obtain licensing to practice their craft openly.

Based on a recipe from 1935, La Clandestine Absinthe Supérieure is a quintessential example of the Swiss-style of clear absinthe that became popular with bootlegging locals following the original ban. Distilled from grain spirits and whole botanicals, the liquid pours crystal clear from the blue glass bottle. Upon the addition of water, bluish tinted clouds emerge that seem to fulfill the spirit's nickname, La Bleue. The aroma yielded from the glass is sweet and earthy. At "only" 106 proof, the relatively mild alcohol content means more seasoned palates will likely be content by adding only 1 to 1$\frac{1}{2}$ volumes of iced water. Anise and fennel present themselves immediately upon sipping, with the sweetness of the anise overlapping woody absinthe notes that arrive in the mid-palate. Additional aromatic herbal notes arise from the mix immediately thereafter, rounding out the mid-palate and persisting through the finish, which while soft, is most refreshing.

– T.A. Breaux

LA CLANDESTINE ABSINTHE SUPÉRIEURE

53% ABV
Distillerie Artemisia-Bugnon
Couvet, Switzerland
www.absinthe-suisse.com

LA FÉE PARISIENNE ABSINTHE SUPÉRIEURE

68% ABV
Green Utopia Ltd.
Cherry Rocher Distillery
Paris, France
www.lafeeabsinthe.com

La Fée Parisienne Absinthe Supérieure is owned by UK-based Green Utopia, Ltd., and crafted near Paris by the Cherry Rocher distillery. In 1999, founder and owner George Rowley approached renowned French author and Absinthe Museum director Marie-Claude Delahaye about the prospect of producing a French answer to the substandard Czech products that prevailed at the time, the result of this collaboration being La Fée Parisienne, which was launched in 2000. Rowley and Delahaye have since worked with Cherry Rocher to further improve the quality and historical accuracy of La Fée Parisienne, releasing a revised bottling that is 100% natural in construction, while also adding craft-distilled La Fée Absinthe Blanche to complement the artisanal French and Swiss Extra Supérieure (XS) range in the portfolio.

La Fée Parisienne is bottled at 68% ABV, the bottle itself being coated with a UV filter to protect the natural color from light. The herb bill for the distillation and coloration of La Fée Parisienne includes grand absinthe, green anise, star anise, sweet fennel, coriander, hyssop, and others that are undisclosed. Instead of combining herbs in the pot and distilling, botanicals used for this absinthe are distilled individually, the resulting distillates blended to achieve better consistency. The spirit pours as a light golden-olive liquid. Seasoned palates should start at 2 to $2\frac{1}{2}$ volumes of iced water, where a cloudy opacity ensues, releasing a soft aroma that is floral and sweet. On the palate, the initial impression is green anise and fennel, with the woody sweetness of star anise also making its presence known, albeit unobtrusively. The initial wave gives way to a slight bitterness from grand absinthe and soft meadow herbs that persist through the finish.

– T.A. Breaux

La Maison Fontaine Absinthe Blanche is the brainchild of Sven Olsen of Taipei and Mark Stringer of London, who created their flagship French blanche as a fashionable answer to the numerous Swiss La Bleue absinthes that have emerged on the European market since the repeal of the Swiss ban in 2005. Having sought the advice of longtime absinthe expert David Nathan-Maister, Olsen and Stringer worked with the respected Distillerie les Fils d'Emile Pernot in Pontarlier, France to perfect a recipe with both traditional roots and suitability to modern mixology. Since the initial launch in 2010, La Maison Fontaine has also added a verte absinthe, as well as a unique chocolate liqueur distilled with grand wormwood from Pontarlier.

La Maison Fontaine Absinthe Blanche is bottled at 56% ABV in clear glass. The herb bill for this absinthe includes some fifteen different botanicals, including Pontarlier grand absinthe, green anise, sweet fennel, chamomile, and quite a few others that remain secret and add to the mix. The spirit pours crystal clear from the bottle, and exudes a soft, sweet aroma. This blanche absinthe louches quickly, and therefore seasoned palates will find 2 to 2 1/2 volumes of iced water as a good starting point. Upon louching, the initially sweet aroma evolves a mild fennel kick. The initial flavors include Pontarlier absinthe with anise and fennel present. Immediately thereafter comes an amalgam of both powdery and piquant herbal notes, including mint, lemon, and floral undertones that persist through a moderately spicy finish.

— T.A. Breaux

LUCID ABSINTHE SUPÉRIEURE

62% ABV
Hood River Distillers
Combier Distillery
Saumur, France
www.drinklucid.com

Lucid Absinthe Supérieure was created for Viridian Spirits by T.A. Breaux in an effort to overturn the longstanding US ban on absinthe. Lucid was developed as a genuine absinthe that would, with the backing of contemporary science and well-constructed legal arguments, present a strong case for approval for the US market. Handcrafted in France at the historic Combier distillery and distilled true to tradition with a full measure of grand absinthe, Lucid became the first genuine absinthe to be imported and distributed in the United States in almost a century. Now under the ownership and guidance of Oregon-based Hood River distillers, Lucid continues to be a cornerstone of the category in the US market.

Lucid was the first absinthe to hit American shelves upon the relegalization of absinthe in the United States in 2007. It's bottled at 62% ABV, and sports a recently revamped logo and embossed green bottle. An inviting shade of green, the aromas of the beet base mingle with fresh herbs, sweet anise, and hints of green tea and Juicy Fruit gum. The louche builds slowly but is still fully developed by 1:1 and ends up with a bright, almost white final product with shades of green throughout. Flavor is herbal and well balanced with a piquant white pepper kick and just the slightest hint of celery. The sweetness of the anise plays nicely with hints of earth and minerals. The finish is slightly dry with an underlying anise sweetness.

– Brian Robinson

The Delaware Phoenix distillery is operated by proprietor/distiller Chery Lins, who performs her craft in the town of Walton, located in rural upstate New York. Cheryl makes no bones about warning prospective buyers that her various whiskeys and absinthes are entirely made by a girl and her copper pot still, and that in no way should a distiller's expertise be judged by a presence of facial hair. From mashing to fermentation to distilling to filling whiskey barrels, Cheryl does it all... inarguably well. It's by no accident that Cheryl's work is acclaimed as a solid example of fine craft distillation in the contemporary market.

Meadow of Love Absinthe Supérieure is described by distiller Cheryl Lins as her "feminine absinthe," as opposed to her Walton Waters brand being her "masculine absinthe" and Blues Cat being a collaborative effort with long-time absinthe experts Artemis and Eric Pryzgocki. Meadow of Love is crafted from grand absinthe, green anise, sweet fennel, Roman wormwood, hyssop, lemon balm, and violet. Its light-olive tint is fairly stable, no doubt due to its robust 68% ABV. When louched with 2 to 2½ parts water, the gold-tinged opaque Meadow of Love gives a powdery floral aroma that rides a backbone of anise. On the palate, the first wave of flavor is a balanced blend of anise, fennel, and absinthe that gradually yields to underlying meadow herbs, including a mild note of violets, that persist through a soft and fairly lengthy finish. The delicate array of flavor effectively disguises the power of the spirit.

– T.A. Breaux

MEADOW OF LOVE ABSINTHE SUPÉRIEURE
68% ABV
Delaware Phoenix Distillery
Walton, New York, USA
www.delawarephoenix.com

PACIFIQUE ABSINTHE VERTE SUPÉRIEURE

68% ABV
Pacific Distillery
Woodinville, Washington, USA
www.pacificdistillery.com

Pacific Distillery is a small, family-owned operation founded by distiller Marc Bernhard in the Seattle suburb of Woodinville. A long-time aficionado of absinthe, Marc launched his distillery with a single copper pot still and having accumulated much information about absinthe crafting through his studies over the years. Marc put those years of research into motion via the release of Pacifique Absinthe Verte Supérieure in 2010, which is based on an 1850s recipe. Some of the botanicals used for both Pacifique as well as the distillery's Voyager Gin are sourced directly from the Bernhard family gardens.

Pacifique Absinthe Verte Supérieure begins with grain neutral spirits, the distillation and coloration being prepared from botanicals such as grand absinthe, green anise, fennel, angelica, coriander, lemon balm, and Roman wormwood. Bottled at 62% ABV, the liquid pours a medium gold-olive tint. Seasoned absintheurs will want to add 2 to 2 ½ volumes of water to get things going, which reveals a green-gold opaque louche. The aroma that wafts from the glass is one of very powdery meadow herbs with an underlayer of anise. On the palate, the initial wave is one of pronounced Roman wormwood and hyssop that gives a dark touch of savory that floats atop a layer of anise and fennel. The strong flavor of the coloring herbs carries into a powdery, herbaceous mid-palate, which descends into lingering notes of citrus and piquant fennel.

– T.A. Breaux

Pernod inherited its name from the long-defunct Pernod Fils company, which closed following the original ban as its only commercial product was absinthe. Today, the Pernod-Ricard company is a huge conglomerate, with a portfolio including numerous whiskeys, vodkas, gins, tequilas, liqueurs, and so forth. Pernod Ricard first re-released its namesake absinthe in 2001, but like many modern specialties the initial release was a product of modern manufacture and ingredients. With the absinthe renaissance and craft cocktail revolution bringing unprecedented interest in artisanal spirits, the big company responded by thinking small. Pernod installed a copper pot still in its Thuir, France, facility for the purpose of bringing its absinthe back to its artisanal roots, which was achieved under the guidance of global brand manager Mathieu Sabbagh, whose family hardware business in Pontarlier was frequented by absinthe bootleggers during the dark days of the ban.

Pernod Absinthe Supérieure is crafted from a base of wine spirit and whole herbs, including the Pontarlier cultivar of grand absinthe, some of which are distilled individually. The liquid that pours from the blue-green glass bottle is a pale olive tint, requiring 2 to 2½ parts water to louche completely. This is where seasoned palates should start. The aroma that wafts from the glass is of soft, powdery anise and fennel. When sipped, the initial flavors include anise, fennel, and a touch of the sweet woody pungency of star anise. In the mid-palate, a mild bitterness with an accompaniment of softer meadow herbs becomes apparent and persists until the finish, where a lasting note of woody star anise lingers. The flavor profile is somewhat softer and lighter than the visibly darker and drier Edition Spéciale 2015 bottling, which delivers distinctly more pronounced herbaceous notes of hyssop and lemon balm.

– T.A. Breaux

PERNOD ABSINTHE SUPÉRIEURE

68% ABV
Pernod Ricard
France
www.pernodabsinthe.com

REDUX ABSINTHE SUPÉRIEURE

65% ABV
Golden Moon Distillery
Golden, Colorado, USA
www.village-distillery.com

Golden Moon distillery was founded in 2008 by absinthe enthusiast Stephen Gould, who is an avid researcher of old and rare books on distillation. With a laundry list of past professions, including saucier, bartender, brewer, and university professor, Gould founded Golden Moon for the purpose of distilling classic staples such as gin, absinthe, grappa, and whiskeys, as well as specialty spirits and liqueurs. Fitted with four antique stills of various provenance, Gould is always working on something new, as well as keeping up with the distillery's busy off-premise tasting room.

Redux Absinthe Supérieure was created by Stephen Gould following years of travels and research. Beginning with a base of grain spirits,

Redux is crafted using the traditional Swiss method and herbs and spices from around the world. Bottled at 65% ABV, Redux is packaged in dark glass to preserve its natural deep olive tint. Seasoned absintheurs will find Redux louched at 2 to 2½ volumes of water. Immediately thereafter emerges an aroma of sweetness and grassy meadow herbs. At first sip appear strong notes of anise and fennel, with a hint of earthy grand absinthe and an accompaniment of meadow herbs, woody sweetness, and a slight hint of mint. Pronounced fennel notes soften as the wave of flavors progresses toward the finish, which leaves a wake of soft, powdery coloring herbs.

— T.A. Breaux

The 1990s and early 2000s saw a rash of Czech "absinths" that amounted to flavored vodkas with green dye, produced by "distilleries" with no distillation equipment, and lacking any characteristics that resembled traditional absinthe. In sharp contrast to this practice is the Žufánek family distillery, founded by Marcela and Josef Žufánek, and run with the help of sons Martin, Josef, and Jan. Located at the foot of the White Carpathian Mountains, the Žufánek distillery possesses four copper stills, and specializes in producing fruit brandies and spirits, liqueurs, and mead from family orchards and apiaries. Absinthe expert Martin Žufánek uses herbs grown on the family farm to create St. Antoine, the first Czech absinthe distilled true to tradition.

St. Antoine Absinthe is bottled at 70% ABV, and begins with grain neutral spirits and traditional botanicals such as grande and Roman wormwood, some of which are cultivated locally. The liquid pours from the brown glass bottle with a medium olive hue. This absinthe louches into a thick opalescent green cloud upon the addition of 2 ½ parts iced water, upon which bold herbaceous aromas emerge. On the palate, the initial flavors tend to be powerful but well balanced, giving prominent notes of grande and petite absinthe, green anise, fennel, and meadow herbs. This wave of botanical strength gradually gives way to a lightly vegetal, lengthy, and mildly anesthetizing finish.

– T.A. Breaux

ST. ANTOINE ABSINTHE
70% ABV
ŽUSY, Ltd.
Boršice u Blatnice, Czech Republic
http://www.zufanek.cz/en

ST. GEORGE ABSINTHE VERTE

60% ABV
St. George Spirits
Alameda, California, USA
www.stgeorgespirits.com

St. George Spirits was founded by now-retired native German Jörg Rupf, who relocated to the San Francisco Bay area in 1982, and began distilling *eau-de-vie* from local fruit. Being an early pioneer in the craft spirits movement, Rupf's proficiency in his art would later attract the attention of master distiller Lance Winters and distiller/blender Dave Smith, who joined Rupf in 1996 and 2005 respectively. Winters had been quietly perfecting his own recipe for absinthe for more than a decade, but it wasn't until the US ban was lifted in March 2007 that commercialization became a possibility. Not wasting any time, St. George Absinthe Verte entered the market later that year, becoming the first American-made absinthe to reach the US market in the post-ban era, becoming an integral element of the various spirits and liqueurs in the St. George portfolio.

Having been conceived in the creative mind of Lance Winters, St. George Absinthe Verte begins with a distillation of star anise, fennel, and grand wormwood in brandy, the distillate being finished with an infusion of an array of whole herbs, including atypical selections such as meadowsweet, tarragon, and stinging nettles. Bottled at a relatively mild 60% in clear glass, St. George is ever present in a dark honeyed-amber *feuille-morte* hue, which confirms what we already know – no artificial colorants are present. Louching with iced water brings forth a dark golden opacity, with an aroma of grassy meadow and a hint of citrus. Seasoned palates will find the addition of 1 1/2 to 2 volumes of water to be enjoyable, the stronger side of the spectrum being preferable. Woody star anise, mint, and earth are evident in the entry, with the mid-palate yielding a mélange of meadow herbs that along with mint and a hint of citrus persist well into the finish. The flavor profile of St. George adds diversity to a traditional theme much like new western gins have to London-style gins.

– T.A. Breaux

Tenneyson Absinthe Royale was jointly formulated by David Nathan-Maister, author of *The Absinthe Encyclopedia*, and American absinthe aficionado Graham Wasilition, and is produced by distiller Dominique Rousselet in the historic Distillerie Les Fils d'Emile Pernot, near Pontarlier, France. Tenneyson is crafted using the distillery's century-old Egrot copper alembics, which are fed a steady diet of locally crafted botanicals and congener-free beet neutral spirits. Wasilition remains the US importer and brand manager for the spirit.

Tenneyson Absinthe Royale is a clear absinthe bottled at 53% ABV, much in the fashion of a Swiss style, La Bleue. The liquid pours crystal clear from the bottle, and gives a full, cloudy louche with 1 to 1 1/2 volumes of iced water, which is where experienced absintheurs will want to start. The aroma wafting from the glass is one of green anise with distinct notes of juniper and citrus. Tasting the liquor brings about anise and fennel up front, with a continuation of the juniper and citrus notes that appeared in the nose. There is a hint of woody sweetness that appears mid-palate, which persists along with the distinct gin-like notes through the finish. Tenneyson may give the appearance of a Swiss La Bleue, but it carries a markedly different attitude.

– T.A. Breaux

TENNEYSON
ABSINTHE ROYALE
53% ABV
Distillerie les Fils d'Emile Pernot
Pontarlier, France
www.tenneyson.com

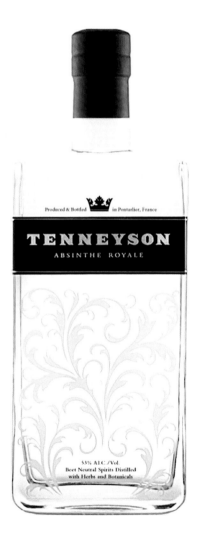

VIEUX CARRÉ ABSINTHE SUPÉRIEURE

60% ABV
Philadelphia Distilling
Philadelphia, Pennsylvania, USA
www.philadelphiadistilling.com

Having arisen as the first distillery in Pennsylvania since Prohibition, Philadelphia Distilling made a splash in 2006 with their distinctly American Bluecoat Gin. Under the direction of distiller Robert Cassel, and guidance of partners Andrew Auwerda and Timothy Yarnall, Philadelphia Distilling made ample use of its Scottish copper pot still, having released vodkas, whiskeys, and seasoned versions thereof, as well as Vieux Carré Absinthe Supérieure, which having been released on the last day of 2008, became the first American absinthe distilled east of the Rockies since the original ban. The name represents a tribute to the Vieux Carré (French Quarter) of New Orleans, the original absinthe capital of the New World.

Vieux Carré Absinthe Supérieure carries an herb bill that includes grand absinthe, green anise, star anise, sweet fennel, Roman wormwood, lemon balm, hyssop, spearmint, and génépi, and is crafted via what is described as a "double maceration" process prior to distillation. The spirit is robustly colored, giving a strong feuille morte hue that comes as a result of its moderate 60% ABV and clear glass bottle. When poured into the glass, the color is a deep gold tint, not unlike a typical VSOP cognac. When louched with 2 volumes of iced water, the spirit becomes a thick golden cloud, yielding an aroma of grassy meadow with undertones of mint. Upon tasting, the woody notes of star anise are apparent, accompanied by anise, fennel, absinthe, and a wealth of balanced herbal aromatics with the pleasant minty note ever present. The finish yields a woody sweetness with more integrated grassy meadow herbs that fade into a lingering wisp of earthy mint.

– T.A. Breaux

VIEUX PONTARLIER
ABSINTHE FRANÇAISE
SUPÉRIEURE

65% ABV
Distillerie les Fils d'Emile Pernot
Pontarlier, France
www.tempusfugitspirits.com/vieux-
pontarlier-absinthe

Vieux Pontarlier Absinthe Française Supérieure was first launched in 2002 by one of the last original absinthe distilleries in the Pontarlier region, Distillerie les Fils d'Emile Pernot. Upon its debut, Vieux Pontarlier represented a departure from the cheaply made, artificially colored absinthes that littered the European market. Vieux Pontarlier has further evolved over the years thanks to the efforts of longtime American absintheur Peter Schaf, who has further honed the quality and historical accuracy of the brand since its initial release. Schaf and partner John Troia founded US-based Tempus Fugit Spirits, which has released several artisanal bitters and liqueurs of historical provenance, and features Vieux Pontarlier prominently its absinthe portfolio.

Vieux Pontarlier Absinthe Française Supérieure is constructed from a base of grape *eau-de-vie*, grande absinthe from Pontarlier, green anise, sweet fennel, and other classic herbs. The spirit pours bright olive green from its dark glass bottle, and requires 2 to 2½ parts water before forming a thick green louche. The aromas that emanate from the glass are somewhat minty and pleasantly vegetal. On the palate, the initial impression is one of a lighter, floral body of green anise, fennel, and absinthe that are well balanced with a hint of bitterness that offsets the sweetness of the anise. The flavors progress with integrated herbaceous notes that appear mid-palate, and linger through a slightly sweet and piquant finish.

– T.A. Breaux

VILYA SPIRITS ABSINTHE SUPERIOR VERTE

68% ABV
Cascadia Artisan Distillery
Cave Junction, Oregon USA
www.cascadiadistillery.net

Vilya Spirits emerged as a collaboration between Joe Legate, the founder of Ridge Distillery, and Jazper Torres, a naturopathic physician, both being longtime absinthe connoisseurs. While Legate initiated distillery operations in hills of Montana, Torres was busy sourcing the native grand absinthe local to the region, as well as wildcrafting other botanicals for the absinthes and gin. With Legate stepping away from the demands of distillery work to spend time with family and pursue other interests, Torres has taken the reins, having relocated the distillery to the Oregon Cascades, and changing the name to Vilya Spirits. With both a verte and blanche absinthe in the portfolio, Torres keeps busy between cultivating plants and distilling them.

Vilya Spirits Absinthe Superior Verte begins with grain neutral spirits, to which botanicals such as grand absinthe, green anise, fennel, coriander, angelica, and elecampane are added, and distilled using a copper pot alembic. The liquor pours a light, golden olive tint, to which seasoned absintheurs will want to add 2 to 2$\frac{1}{2}$ volumes of ice water for tasting. Upon doing so, a thick golden louche develops, yielding an aroma of soft, grassy meadow herbs. Tasting sets off a well-integrated blend of absinthe, anise, and fennel. The mid-palate brings forth a bit more fennel as well as the more piquant herbs, which softens into a mild grassy finish.

– T.A. Breaux

Select Bibliography

Conrad, Barnaby. *Absinthe: History in a Bottle.* San Francisco: Chronicle Books, 1997.

Crowley, Aleister. *Absinthe: The Green Goddess.* Edmonds, WA: Holmes Pub. Group, 1994.

Delahaye, Marie-Claude. *L'Absinthe: Art et Histoire.* Paris: Trame Way, 1990.

    L'absinthe: Histoire de la Fée verte. Paris: Berger-Levrault, 1983.

    L'absinthe: Les cuillères. Auvers-sur-Oise: Absinthe Museum, 2001.

    L'absinthe: Muse des poètes. Auvers-sur-Oise: Absinthe Museum, 2000.

    L'Absinthe: Son Histoire. Auvers-sur-Oise: Absinthe Museum, 2001.

Delahaye, Marie-Claude, and Benoît Noël. *Absinthe: Muse des Peintres.* Paris: L'Amateur, 1999.

Rimbaud, Jean-Nicolas Arthur, trans. Mark Spitzer. *From Absinthe to Abyssinia: Selected Miscellaneous, Obscure and Previously Untranslated Works of Jean-Nicolas-Arthur Rimbaud.* Berkeley, CA: Creative Arts Books, 2002.

Betina J. Wittels

Betina J. Wittels, Ms Ed, cofounded a shelter for runaways in 1976, which is still in operation today. She has maintained a private practice in adolescent, marital, and family therapy for four decades.

Creator of the website www.allthingsabsinthe.com, Betina was one of the first to formally introduce absinthe antiques into the United States more than twenty years ago.

Sojourning on ships throughout the world since age three, the gypsy wanderlust has never ceased to flow in Wittels' veins. Passionate for life, she is willing to turn over any boulder or slip into any barrio to uncover a rare spoon or a bottle of vintage absinthe. And, of course, she possesses a white wolf dog and a black cat. The green fairy comes and goes as she pleases.

The wolf howls and protects, the cat purrs and soothes, and the green fairy beckons her to write the words in this book.

Betina is photographed in front of an original 1902 lithograph, created by the Mourgue brothers during the height of Absinthe's rage. Measuring 3.5 x 5 feet, only two exist in the world. One is owned by the grandson of Bourgeois, while Betina owns the second. When she purchased it, it was folded and covered in dust but wiping it with a dry, clean cloth revealed vivid, fresh colors.

T.A. Breaux

T.A. Breaux is a native New Orleanian and research scientist who has dedicated more than twenty years of research toward resolving the mysteries and myths associated with absinthe. His mission to painstakingly reconstruct historically accurate examples of the controversial spirit gave rise to Jade Liqueurs (www.jadeliqueurs.com).

Breaux codirected the effort to lift the United State's 95-year ban on absinthe. The following year, Breaux was similarly engaged in reversing the last vestiges of the original French ban, which allowed absinthe to be formally recognized in that country. His work has been lauded throughout the press and media in the US, Europe, and Australia since 2000, including numerous national television appearances (The History Channel, Discovery Channel, CBS, MSNBC, Travel Channel, PBS, etc.).

Breaux has co-authored and published scientific studies on vintage absinthe in peer-reviewed journals (*Journal of Agricultural and Food Science*). Breaux's reputation for being a staunch promoter of truth and accuracy of information and education in all matters absinthe is surpassed only by his limitless passion for recreating history through the fine art of absinthe crafting.

FULCRUM